FOR MY PARENTS
NICHOLAS AND VICTORIA,
AND, ABOVE ALL, FOR MY
WONDERFUL SISTER HOLLY,
WHO PUTS EVERYTHING
INTO PERSPECTIVE

QUADRILLE

Photography by
Sasha Wilkins

Additional photography
by Lisa Linder

FRIENDS
FOOD
FAMILY

ESSENTIAL RECIPES, TIPS, AND SECRETS
FOR THE MODERN HOSTESS FROM
LIBERTYLONDONGIRL.COM

SASHA WILKINS

COOKERY NOTES

• Butter is salted unless otherwise stated.

• Eggs are large unless otherwise stated, and I always recommend using free-range, organic eggs whenever possible.

• I recommend using unwaxed citrus fruits when grating the zest.

• Recipes were tested in a convection oven. If using a regular oven, follow manufacturer's advice for adjusting temperatures.

• 1 Tbsp (tablespoon) is equal to 3 tsp.

• All salt is kosher salt unless otherwise stated.

Publishing Director: Jane O'Shea
Creative Director: Helen Lewis
Senior Editor: Céline Hughes
Designer: Nicola Ellis
Illustrator: Heather Gately
Photographers: Sasha Wilkins and Lisa Linder
Prop Stylist for Special Photography: Iris Bromet
Production: Vincent Smith, Sasha Hawkes

First published in 2014 by
Quadrille Publishing Limited
Pentagon House
52–54 Southwark Street
London SE1 1UN
www.quadrille.co.uk

Quadrille is an imprint of Hardie Grant.
www.hardiegrant.com.au

Cataloguing in Publication Data: a catalogue record for this book is available from the British Library.

ISBN: 978 184949 661 2

Printed in China

CONTENTS

SECRETS OF SUCCESSFUL ENTERTAINING

Nothing has surprised me more than the success of my blog LibertyLondonGirl. It was only ever meant to be my diary when I moved from London to New York back in 2007, so that my family and friends could stay up to date with my new life in America.

Much to my initial surprise, the subject of food and entertaining has always been one of the most popular threads across all of LibertyLondonGirl, from advice posts —maybe the best place to buy cannoli in Manhattan's Little Italy—to copious recipes, always developed by me, and usually inspired by what I found in the market or in my fridge that day, via Instagrams of table settings.

When it comes to the food part, I am not a chef: I am a cook. And I have been since the age of four when my mother first taught me how to roll out pastry, with a tiny wooden rolling pin from my Galt children's baking set, a present from my godmother Rachel. Thanks to them, it seemed natural to spend as much time as I could in the kitchen when I was growing up, and so all my earliest memories (from the 1970s) revolve around food.

Those memories include watching my mother make chicken liver pâtés in deep stoneware bowls to sell in the local deli; coming home from school on Wednesday to discover every kitchen surface covered in wire racks of cooling cakes and cookies from Delia Smith's *Book of Cakes*; the endless files of cut-out newspaper recipes to thumb through by Marika Hanbury-Tenison, Katie Stewart, Jane Grigson, Josceline Dimbleby, Caroline Conran et al.; and packed lunches that my school friends thought bizarre, including chunks of fresh mozzarella cheese, cold slices of gratins, homemade pizza, and olives.

So it's not surprising that I equate food with happiness, and that feeding my friends and family is my favorite occupation.

Wherever I find myself in the world, I cook for my friends and the people that I meet along the way. Of course, it's a challenge: getting used to new kitchens, different ingredients, cooking with whatever you can find. On my last road trip in California, I traveled with a box of kitchen essentials in the trunk of my car, and I will never forget sugar pouring out of a pocket in my backpack on the luggage rack onto a passenger's head on an overnight coach journey in Australia. Some of my most memorable meals have been cooked in the most unexpected places: a youth hostel by the Golden Gate Bridge with raccoons sitting by the window, a friend's house right on Venice Beach, a children's home in Singapore, a hotel kitchen in New Delhi.

My biggest culinary shock was New York. I'd heard all the stories about Manhattan kitchens and their shoebox proportions, but nothing really prepares you for a cooking space less than a yard wide—and that includes the storage. It was a real test. Not least because I'd designed and had fitted my perfect London kitchen just a year before I moved to New York. But I learned to adapt, and honed my recipes so that they could be prepared with minimum fuss—and with the minimum of kitchen tools.

Now I am based back in London, I once again have my collection of cooking equipment around me so I can feed people on a far larger scale. Because we eat. And eat properly. I utterly refute the cry of "nothing tastes as good as skinny feels." Goodness, life would be so unutterably boring without delicious things to eat. I find it hard to admire

people who pick at food, or remain resolutely opposed to eating.

Don't get me wrong; I watch my weight as much as the next person (there's a fine dividing line between perky and porky), but food should be a pleasure. And I hope that is what readers will take away from this book.

My hope is that the book will help the reader rustle up a meal anywhere from a beach house in Cornwall to a youth hostel kitchen somewhere idyllic, via the tiniest of Manhattan apartments, whether using food from the back of the fridge or from a fancy food market, all the while making the people around the table feel relaxed, happy, and well fed.

I'm not into napkin origami, and I don't obsess about matching plates. I am as likely to serve my cakes as fat slices wrapped in wax paper, as am I am to decorate them with crystallized violets on a vintage cake stand. My soups work just as well in a thermos up a mountain, as they do in porcelain bowls with matching saucers.

Above all, I believe that it is the atmosphere that we create around our food that matters, not the place or the manner in which it is served (although that's not to say that I don't love a starched tablecloth when one comes my way).

I am definitely the modern type of hostess: I run my own home, I live alone, and I earn my own money, but I don't think there's anything wrong with embracing domesticity; with making people feel comfortable in the environment you create around them. Whether that environment has flowers picked from your garden and plonked in a jug, or the result of spending hours at a flower market and arranging perfect vases, the net result is that a happy host when entertaining makes for happy guests.

I cannot abide the kind of home entertaining that requires four different kinds of fork and plates of food that have been endlessly tweaked and smeared and garnished. Most people are just deliriously happy to be fed by someone else, and if they wanted Michelin grandeur, then they would be sitting in a starred establishment in a party dress, not lolling around a friend's kitchen table, sucking up a Bloody Mary and gossiping.

So I like to serve simple food, using carefully thought out ingredients that allow me to spend as much time talking to my friends and family as I do sweating over the stove.

It always worries me when people say they don't know how to cook. It shouldn't be treated like rocket science: it's just food, the stuff we eat each and every day to keep us strong and healthy. Likewise, when I see friends and readers get into a state about entertaining: a few simple tricks and I hope you will never worry again about the color of your napkins or candles.

I draw the line at ready-made meals, and processed food (beyond baked beans and ramen noodles when truly desperate) doesn't appeal to me, so even when I am running around like a headless chicken, I try to throw something together. On an average day, I set a limit of twenty minutes for prep and cooking, and it's surprising how much you can make in that time frame.

I don't pretend to have all the answers in the kitchen and in the dining room. But what I do have is a headful of recipes, and ways to serve up delicious food that is kind to your body and to your budget.

BREAKFASTS, BRUNCHES, AND BURGERS

I never really understood brunch until I moved to Manhattan, where brunch isn't just a meal—it's a way of life. There are blogs and books dedicated to charting the best places to grab your eggs, and New Yorkers think nothing of lining up for as long as an hour to eat at the latest hot spot.

That being said, I do not love brunch in New York restaurants. It's not the ritual that's at fault, but the mediocre food served by restaurants that have no business to be serving Eggs Benedict and Mimosas, at vastly inflated prices, to endless lines of grumpy, hungry people. Even the couscous place opposite my old St Mark's Place apartment was at it.

Never will I understand the New Yorker's fervent desire to stand in a line for 60 minutes just to eat, in a city that has a restaurant every 50 yards. Insanity.

But I do love meeting friends at the weekend for leisurely, late breakfasts that morph into lunches; the buzz and the chatter; the paper-reading and the Bloody Marys. So, my solution to avoid standing in line is to cook it myself.

Breakfast is possibly my favorite meal of the day (I always wake up with a rumbling stomach) and I've never drawn a line in the menu over what makes suitable morning food. I loved living in Singapore where breakfast is so often a bowl of chili-spiked noodles. That's probably why the concept of brunch is so appealing: I can eat whatever I want, and still think of it as breakfast.

I think my love of breakfast is partly down to my fascination with American diners, where the definition of breakfast is also elastic. Whether you want a classic burger, or a short stack of pancakes, granola, or waffles and whipped cream, a diner can and will serve you.

In this chapter I've pulled together a few of my favorite breakfast and brunch ideas, and because so many of them are inspired by the food I've eaten in American diners, there's my homage to the diner, too.

BUTTERMILK PANCAKES

We never had pancakes for breakfast, growing up, but my five years in America introduced me to the joy of a short stack with melted butter, syrup cascading down the sides, and berries and powdered sugar decorating the whole. It's a fine way to start the day. If you really wanted to go the whole American hog, then strips of very crispy bacon would not go astray either.

Pancakes are perfect for serving to large mixed groups, as both children and adults love them. I have seen plenty of parents stealing bits from their kids' plates when they think no one is watching.

If you get cracking just before everyone sits down, then you will thank yourself, because most people will eat at least three of these. Fortunately, they are resilient beasts, and won't suffer too badly if left for a few minutes, while you get on with the rest.

This recipe makes 10 to 12 pancakes, based on a size of 3 to 4 inches [8 to 10 cm] across.

MAKES 10 TO 12

2 eggs
1 cup [240 ml] buttermilk
1⅓ cups + 1 Tbsp [175 g]
  all-purpose flour
Pinch of salt
1 heaping tsp baking
  powder
4 Tbsp sunflower oil

SECRET
If you don't have buttermilk at home, simply mix 1 Tbsp lemon juice into ¾ cup [175 ml] whole milk.

METHOD

It's the work of moments to prepare the batter, which you can do the night before. Beat together the eggs and the buttermilk, or milk and lemon juice. Sift together the dry ingredients in a separate bowl. Now add the liquid ingredients to the sifted dry ones, and whisk together with a balloon whisk until smooth.

Add the oil to a frying pan and heat. Spoon the batter into the pan to make a circle about 3½ in [9 cm] in diameter. Don't make more than 2 or 3 simultaneously, as the oil temperature will drop and the pancakes will be soggy.

Flip the pancakes when the tops are still liquid, and you can see a few bubbles. These are a practice-makes-perfect thing: after making a couple you'll be able to judge when to do the flip: usually earlier than you might think. You are aiming for a nicely browned bottom.

TOPPINGS

- BLUEBERRIES AND MAPLE SYRUP
- NUTELLA AND BANANAS
- STRAWBERRIES AND WHIPPED CREAM
- APPLESAUCE AND GROUND CINNAMON
- PECANS AND MAPLE SYRUP
- CHOCOLATE CHIPS

1 THE WOLSELEY
160 Piccadilly, W1J 9EB
www.thewolseley.com

2 CECCONI'S
5A Burlington Gardens, W1S 3EP
www.cecconis.co.uk

3 DEAN STREET TOWNHOUSE
69–71 Dean Street, W1D 3SE
www.deanstreettownhouse.com

4 BALTHAZAR
6 Russell Street, WC2B 5HZ
www.balthazarlondon.com

5 THE DELAUNAY
55 Aldwych, WC2B 4BB
www.thedelaunay.com

FIVE LONDON RESTAURANTS
for smart breakfasts

FRENCH BROCANTES

Spending several weeks each summer in rural France, in the Vienne, has given me a passion for French junk shops and the **brocantes** (vintage markets) and **vide-greniers** (literally, empty-attics) that pop up most weekends. Keep an eye out when in the car, as they are often advertised with curbside placards. **www.vide-greniers.org** also covers brocantes and marchés aux puces (flea markets). It's an excellent resource and handy for checking out what's on when.

My favorite secret junk shop is the **Dépôt-Vente La Fauvette** in Châtellerault, France which has almost 1000 square feet of, well, second-hand everything, including china and glass.

35 rue Jean de la Fontaine, 86100 Châtellerault, Vienne; open Thursday, Friday and Saturday 9:30 A.M. to 12 P.M. and 2:30 P.M. to 7 P.M.; Sunday 2:30 P.M. to 7 P.M.; www.depot-vente-la-fauvette.fr

Just a block from the seafront, the alluring flower and food markets on the pretty **Cours Saleya in old Nice** make space for an antiques-and-vintage market every Monday. It's particularly good for traditional ceramics, travel ephemera, and prints.

Open Monday 6 A.M. to 6 P.M.

Les Puces du Canal, France's second biggest flea market, just outside Lyon, has a mixture of indoor permanent stands, and outdoor stalls. Given its regional setting, it's the place to pick up horticultural and outdoor collectables.

1 rue du Canal, 69100 Villeurbanne, Lyons; open Thursday and Saturday 7 A.M. to 12 P.M., Sunday 7 A.M. to 2 P.M.; www.pucesducanal.com

POMEGRANATE, PLUM, AND YOGURT PARFAITS

I love fall; it's my favorite season. Wrapped up in warm clothes, but with the sun still shining, I tramp around London's parks with the sausage dog prancing in front, looking forward to eating soups and cake and pies and plums.

Which brings me to my autumnal breakfast.

I eat yogurt every day: in the summer with peaches and strawberries; in fall with blackberries and plums and pomegranates. I add rolled oats, nuts, and seeds. (Granola is great. Try my no-raisin take on page 16).

It may seem like I'm just filling space by writing a recipe for something as simple as a dish of yogurt and fruit for breakfast. But if you can spend five minutes, instead of three, layering it all up in a glass, then you have something truly delightful as opposed to just all right. And, if you are going to focus on eating healthily, it's amazing how much more appetizing a dish can be if it looks good.

In this case, the presentation really does make it taste better. Here's why: layering the ingredients in advance allows the flavors to mingle. The yogurt softens the oats so they become easier to digest, and the plums start to leach their sticky, yellow juice into the yogurt. The sweet ooze of the plums contrasts perfectly with the slightly mouth-puckering, crunchy pomegranate seeds.

SERVES 4
1 pomegranate
2¼ cups [500 g] natural yogurt
1 cup [100 g] rolled oats
3 Tbsp sunflower seeds
4 ripe plums, chopped (Victorias, in an ideal world)

METHOD
Pick 4 pretty water glasses.

The quickest way to remove seeds from a pomegranate is to halve the fruit first. Then take a wooden spoon and bang the outside of each half over a bowl; the seeds will fall out.

In each glass, place a layer of chopped plums, yogurt, oats, and sunflower seeds followed by more yogurt and plums, then top with more oats, sunflower seeds, and the pomegranate seeds. Done.

Leave for 5 to 10 minutes (but overnight would be wonderful) if you can, to let the flavors mingle. If you like, add a drizzle of honey. Your call.

FULL-OF-GOOD-THINGS,
NO-RAISINS GRANOLA

I do not like dried fruit in my granola or muesli, and I'm not a fan of ingesting hundreds of sugar-filled calories in my cereal either. I developed this version for my rather specific tastes, and it turns out that I am not alone, because the first version of this recipe has been enduringly popular on my website. (Of course, if you like dried fruit in your granola, feel free to add it.)

My granola addiction dates back to very recent times. In California's Wine Country for the wedding of my dear friends Jill and Michael, I wandered into a café on Calistoga's main street looking for something breakast-y. There wasn't much on the menu, bar a bowl of granola, so I ordered it. I don't like cereal as a rule, and especially not sweet cereal, so I prepared to grit my teeth. Imagine my surprise when I thoroughly enjoyed my heaping bowl of granola—it was crunchy, unsweetened, and wholly delicious, and now that I have worked out how to make my own, I eat it in shovelfuls.

I often use a package of multigrain muesli mix containing oats, barley, spelt, and toasted rye flakes, but you can easily make your own mix with my suggested ingredients below.

MAKES 7 CUPS [1 KG]

2 Tbsp clear honey
2 Tbsp agave nectar
2 tsp maple syrup
½ cup [120 ml] warm water
¼ cup [60 ml] apple juice
7 cups [1 kg] mixed grains and seeds—I generally use 2¼ cups [300 g] porridge oats, 2¼ cups [300 g] rolled barley flakes, ½ cup [80 g] chopped nuts (almonds, hazelnuts, Brazil nuts, and macadamia nuts are all good), ¾ cup [120 g] sunflower seeds, ¾ cup [120 g] chopped pumpkin seeds, ¼ cup [30 g] ground flaxseeds, and ¼ cup [40 g] chia seeds)

METHOD
Preheat the oven to 250°F [120°C].

In a small saucepan, heat up the honey, agave nectar, maple syrup, and water. Then add the apple juice.

When it's all warm and flowing nicely, pour over your grain mixture, forming it into clumps with your hands. (Clumps are good as they give you extra crunch.) If you eat a bit now and it tastes quite sweet, do not worry—that sweetness disappears upon cooking. It should smell like a warm hamster cage.

Scoop the mixture out onto 2 or 3 large, flat baking pans, squishing it in your hands and making sure it has lots of little clumps and balls. It's important not to have a layer that's too thick, or it won't crisp properly. Bake in the oven for about 45 minutes. Every 15 minutes or so, take the pans out and shake the granola about so that it cooks evenly.

I prefer mine quite brown so it's really crunchy—I recommend tasting as you go to see what you prefer.

That's it. Leave it on the pan to cool, then scoop into sterilized, airtight jars. (See page 114 for more information on sterilizing jars.)

CORN, CHEESE, AND BACON MUFFINS

Savory muffins aren't nearly as common on the European side of the Atlantic as they are in America: when I lived in California, friends would make batches and freeze them, using them as a convenient, on-the-hoof breakfast.

That being said, it's also very satisfying to pull apart a muffin, warm from the oven, and slathering over butter, which then melts down your chin.

MAKES 8
1 Tbsp baking powder
2 cups + 1 Tbsp [250 g] all-purpose flour
3 Tbsp light cream
3 eggs
½ cup [120 g] canned corn kernels
1¼ cups [100 g] grated Monterey Jack or cheddar cheese
2 to 3 slices bacon, snipped into small pieces
Salt and freshly ground black pepper
Muffin pan, lined with 8 paper muffin cups

METHOD
Preheat the oven to 350°F [180°C].

Mix together the baking powder and flour.

In a separate bowl, beat together the cream and eggs with the corn, cheese, and bacon, along with a generous pinch of salt and a grind of black pepper.

In a large mixing bowl, combine all the ingredients.

This is a sticky dough, so it is helpful to use a large ice-cream scoop to measure accurate amounts for each muffin. Divide the mixture between the paper cups and bake for 20 minutes.

Remove the muffins from the pan and allow to cool on a wire rack.

SECRET
Try switching around the fillings: I love spinach and feta cheese, and sun-blush tomatoes and fresh herbs are good, too.

FRENCH TOAST (EGGY BREAD)

French toast has always been a morning classic in my household, whether savory or sweet. Also known as eggy bread (which horrifies my American friend, Steve, who thinks it smacks too much of the nursery so, of course, I delight in only calling it eggy bread in his presence) it is simply fresh or stale bread soaked in seasoned, beaten egg and fried—although I have a suggestion here for baking it, which I prefer.

Count on one egg per slice of bread. Most people will eat two slices (I find guests can be bottomless pits where French toast is concerned).

Break the eggs into a bowl, and beat with a fork. For savory French toast, add a pinch of salt; for sweet, add a heaping teaspoon of white superfine sugar.

Slice the bread thickly, and cut off the crusts. Dip the bread thoroughly in the egg, a piece at a time, making sure it is saturated and soggy with beaten egg. Soak for longer if it is stale or if you like very thick slices.

Add a couple of tablespoons of cooking oil to a large frying pan, and heat it until it smokes. Turn the extractor fan onto high. (This dish is going to spread frying smells everywhere otherwise.) Slide two pieces at a time into the frying pan (too much cools down the oil and the toast will be soggy).

I like French toast quite browned and very crispy, but if you want a lighter color, keep checking the bottom of the bread and then flip it over when done to your liking, to cook the reverse side.

Flip it out of the frying pan and onto paper towels to drain off some of the oil. Arrange beautifully on a plate.

BAKED FRENCH TOAST
I made this by accident one day when I was staring into the frying pan, thinking that it was a shame you needed so much oil to make French toast successfully. Wondering what would happen if I baked it, I put a roasting pan with 2 tablespoons vegetable oil in the oven at 350°F [180°C], to heat.

When the oil was heated, I slipped in four slices of egg-soaked bread and shut the oven door. Imagine my surprise when I checked in ten minutes later to discover my bread all puffed up like a Yorkshire pudding. Success! I checked the bottoms of the slices and discovered delectably crisp bottoms.

Baked French toast is most successful with bread that is extra-thick-sliced—at least 3/4 inch [2 cm]. The longer the soaking time the better—twenty minutes is just perfect.

CORNISH FRENCH TOAST
This is so many ways of righteous wrong. It was an idea born when I was staying in a vacation rental in Cornwall in the UK. Our hosts had left us free-range eggs, bread, jam, and heavy cream. So, when it came to cooking breakfast next morning, I suppose I could have made poached eggs. But I was on vacation, the sun was shining, and that heavy cream was singing a siren song from the fridge. Make your French toast as normal, and then pile on the jam and cream.

INDIAN FRENCH TOAST
This stratospherically wonderful version requires the egg to be beaten with about 2 scant tablespoons [25 ml] milk, a pinch of salt, a finely chopped green chile, and half a chopped onion, then soaking the bread in the mixture before frying.

BAKED EGGS
WITH MUSHROOMS

My grandmother, Granny Horse, had a set of Royal Worcester china egg coddlers when I was a little girl. They fascinated me to the point where she gave in and cooked me a coddled egg. I can't say I was that impressed: essentially, what she served me was an extremely runny poached egg.

Once I could cook for myself I did my own experimenting: a coddled egg is an egg cooked in a closed-top, buttered, china vessel, so it poaches very, very gently and the egg white never goes rubbery. I played around and discovered that I much preferred the French approach—poaching them in a ramekin that is surrounded by water, "en cocotte."

I'm not going to pretend these are a healthy breakfast option. Instead, I'm going to revel in their sheer, indulgent deliciousness: they are very, very rich.

If you aren't keen on mushrooms, simply leave them out. (You could substitute chopped ham.)

SERVES 4

2 cups [250 g] mushrooms
3 scallions
4 tsp [20 g] butter
½ garlic clove, chopped
Handful soft green herbs, chopped (I like chervil, chives, thyme, and oregano), plus extra, to serve
Salt and freshly ground black pepper
4 eggs
3 Tbsp heavy cream
¾ cup [50 g] grated Parmesan cheese
4 slices of toast, to serve
4 ovenproof ramekins

METHOD

Preheat the oven to 350°F [180°C].

Very finely chop the mushrooms and the scallions (use half the green parts), and fry them until soft in a generous amount of butter over medium heat with the garlic and the fresh herbs.

Divide the mixture between 4 ramekins, add salt and pepper, and carefully break an egg over the mushrooms.

Pour over the heavy cream and sprinkle over the grated cheese.

Place the ramekins in a roasting pan and pour boiling water around them to reach ½ in [1 cm] under the lip. Cook for about 10 minutes.

Sprinkle over some black pepper and a few chopped herbs, and eat with toast.

FAVORITE AMERICAN DINERS

SOMETIMES YOU JUST WANT TO SIT
AT A COUNTER AND ORDER COFFEE
AND A BURGER. MAYBE EGGS.
AND POSSIBLY A DANISH ...

B&H DAIRY
127 2nd Avenue, New York

A KOSHER DINER. AND MY OLD MANHATTAN
BREAKFAST HAUNT. STILL OPERATIONAL AFTER
SIXTY-FIVE YEARS IN BUSINESS. IT'S BECOME AN
EAST VILLAGE INSTITUTION. VERY INEXPENSIVE.
THEIR CHALLAH FRENCH TOAST IS WORTH
TRAVELING FOR.

THE 11TH STREET DINER
South Beach, Miami

OPEN 24 HOURS A DAY AND HOUSED IN AN
ORIGINAL ART-DECO DINING CAR. MAKE SURE
YOU ORDER A SIDE OF FLORIDA AVOCADO WITH
EVERYTHING YOU EAT.
WWW.ELEVENTHSTREETDINER.COM

SWINGERS DINER
*820 Beverly Boulevard,
Los Angeles*

SIT AT THE COUNTER AT THIS TRADITIONAL DINER
IN THE HEART OF BEVERLY HILLS. AND ENJOY SOME
GRADE-A PEOPLE-WATCHING: ACTORS. LOVERS.
GRANNIES. DATES ... WWW.SWINGERSDINER.COM

IT'S TOPS COFFEE SHOP
*1801 Market Street,
San Francisco*

I'M NOT SURE WHETHER I LOVE THE NAME OR THE
PEPTO-BISMOL-PINK WAITRESS UNIFORMS MORE ...
WWW.ITSTOPSCOFFEESHOP.COM

EGGS WITH CHICKPEA PUREE AND FLATBREAD

I ate something similar to this for breakfast in Marrakesh, and fell hard for the earthiness of chickpeas against creamy, runny eggs, whether scrambled, fried, or poached. Chili sauce would be more than acceptable here, too. For a delicious, quick, satisfying breakfast, this is hard to beat.

SERVES 2

1 cup [240 g] canned chickpeas
  (reserve some liquid from the can)
2 Tbsp olive oil
1 garlic clove, peeled
Good handful cilantro or
  flat-leaf parsley leaves, chopped
Salt and freshly ground black pepper
4 eggs
2 large flatbreads

METHOD

In a food processor, whizz up the chickpeas with a little of the liquid from their can, 1 Tbsp of the olive oil, the garlic, some of the herbs, and some salt and pepper.

Now choose how to cook your eggs, whether fried (as pictured above), poached (see page 26), or as follows: in a frying pan, heat the rest of the olive oil, break in the eggs and gently stir with a fork until lightly cooked. (They aren't supposed to be scrambled; more like a cross between fried eggs and an omelet.)

To serve, put a dollop of the chickpea purée on the plate, slide on the eggs, and garnish with some of the herbs. Serve with the flatbreads.

FIVE LONDON RESTAURANTS AND CAFES FOR BRUNCH

THE BREAKFAST CLUB
(Soho, Angel, Hoxton, Spitalfields, Battersea Rise and London Bridge)
www.thebreakfastclubcafes.com

THE RIDING HOUSE CAFE
43–51 Great Titchfield Street, W1W 7PQ
www.ridinghousecafe.co.uk

KOPAPA
32–34 Monmouth Street, WC2H 9HA
www.kopapa.co.uk

THE MODERN PANTRY
47–48 St John's Square, EC1V 4JJ
www.themodernpantry.co.uk

LANTANA
13 Charlotte Place, W1T 1SN
www.lantanacafe.co.uk

SATURDAY MORNING OMELET TORTILLA WRAP

I eat these the morning after the night before: they are filling, very savory for a deadened palate, quite low in carbs, and packed full of vegetables and protein in a not-too-worthy manner.

They are simply two-egg omelets, topped with mushrooms, scallions, and cheese, rolled up in a tortilla and eaten with fingers—and gusto.

METHOD

Heat 1 Tbsp of the olive oil in a small frying pan and gently cook the mushrooms and the scallions until soft. Season with salt and black pepper.

Reserve on a plate. Put a little more oil in the empty mushroom pan.

Beat the eggs and season with salt and black pepper before pouring into the pan. Let the bottom set, and then use a fork to lift the edges and swirl the uncooked egg underneath to set. (This is a very thin omelet.)

When the top looks cooked, add the mushrooms and scallions. Scatter the cheese and chopped chives over the top.

Heat up a second frying pan, place a tortilla in it, and slide in the cooked omelet over the tortilla.

After a minute or so, when the tortilla is both warm and softened by the heat, slide it onto a plate and roll up. Then take a very sharp, non-serrated knife, and cut into 3 pieces.

I like to eat these with ample amounts of Sriracha chili sauce.

SERVES 1

1 to 2 Tbsp olive oil
5 mushrooms, sliced
2 scallions, sliced diagonally
Salt and freshly ground black pepper
2 eggs
½ cup [50 g] grated hard cheese, or soft cheese (any cheese will do really)
1 Tbsp chopped chives
1 medium tortilla

HUEVOS RANCHEROS

While I am a strong advocate of a big platter of food in the center of the table that my guests can dive into, helping themselves to the bits that they favor, there are some dishes that just work better one-on-one, so to speak.

Huevos rancheros, with its piled-high layering of tortilla, salsa, beans, avocado, and fried eggs is the perfect individual plate: colorful, appealing, and delicious. That being said, I've eaten some unappealing versions, some reduced to just eggs, salsa, and tortilla; others ruined by pallid yolks, watery tomatoes, or tasteless beans. Like any simple dish—it takes a scant 30 minutes to prep and cook—huevos rancheros only works when the ingredients are good in the first place.

I'm not going to pretend this is an echt huevos rancheros. But it tastes damn good, looks delicious (sometimes this dish can look like roadkill), and has all the key ingredients. I've purposely kept the chili count low because so many people don't like the burn, but that's nothing a good dash of hot sauce can't put right.

SERVES 4
6 medium tomatoes
1 small onion
Bunch cilantro leaves, chopped
1 lime
Salt and freshly ground black
  pepper
Oil, for frying
2 tsp ground cumin
1 garlic clove, crushed
1 cup [240 g] canned pinto or
  black beans, or refried beans
Tabasco or hot sauce
4 tortillas
4 to 8 large eggs
2 packed cups [200 g] grated
  cheese (I use Monterey Jack,
  otherwise cheddar will do)
½ cup [125 g] sour cream
Four-Minute Guacamole
  (see page 170)

METHOD
Roughly chop the tomatoes, removing their cores, and finely chop the onion. Add to a bowl with about 1 Tbsp of the chopped cilantro, a squeeze of lime, and a little salt, and mix together.

Heat 2 tsp olive oil, add the cumin, and fry for a few seconds, before adding the crushed garlic, beans, enough water to fill half the empty can, and a dash of Tabasco or hot sauce. Mix together thoroughly, mashing the beans, and simmer away gently until everything else is ready.

Heat each tortilla in a dry frying pan for 1 minute or so each side, until they start to puff and brown. Reserve in a warm oven or at the back of the stove.

Finally, fry 1 to 2 eggs per person, depending on greed.

To serve, put a warm tortilla on each plate. Spoon over the beans and the tomato salsa, side by side.

Sprinkle over the grated cheese and slide on the fried eggs.

Put a very large dollop of sour cream on one side and the same of guacamole on the other. Liberally sprinkle with chopped cilantro. Eat.

SECRET
This goes very well
with Bloody Marys.

ESSENTIAL
KITCHEN EQUIPMENT

While most cooks could produce delicious things from their kitchen with just a frying pan, saucepan, cutting board, a single sharp knife, and a wooden spoon, there are some bits of kit that do make life a lot easier. Things like rolling pins can always be subbed: milk bottles work well, but try cooling a cake without a wire rack ...

THESE ARE THE POSSESSIONS I USE THE MOST:

- A digital timer and thermometer combined
- A 7-inch [18-cm] nonstick cake pan
- Tongs
- A mandoline for slicing things very thinly
- A stand mixer—for cake batters and frosting
- A food processor for grating, chopping, and puréeing
- A wire rack for cooling cakes and cookies
- A wide and high straight-sided frying pan— a sauteuse
- Silicone spatulas
- A good vegetable peeler and an apple corer
- Measuring spoons and cups
- A tiny whisk for dressings, and a large one for sauces
- A measuring cup with markings
- Digital scales
- A set of stainless steel mixing bowls
- A large sieve—which can double as a colander

I don't use them as often, but a salad spinner, a silicone pastry brush, and a mortar and pestle are great investments.

THE EASIEST POACHED EGGS, WITH SPINACH PURÉE AND ENGLISH MUFFINS

SECRET
Frozen spinach is the secret here. Defrosted, it makes a great sauce when mixed with a little vegetable stock and cream, or crème fraîche.

For anyone reading this who has the fear where poached eggs are concerned, read on: I have found the solution.

For years, poached eggs have been my downfall in the kitchen. I have tried whirlpools, which never whirled enough; vinegar, which made my eggs taste funny; silicone molds, which made my eggs look like discs; and metal poachers which stuck to the eggs ... nothing, nothing worked, neatly proving my point that, however confident you are in the kitchen, there will always be something that is your cook's Achilles heel.

Then I was accidentally served a cold poached egg with my breakfast in a London restaurant and I couldn't for the life of me work out how that had happened. I looked a little closer, realized that my egg resembled a money bag, and it all became clear: they had broken the egg into a ramekin lined with plastic wrap, and then scrunched up the top. That meant they could poach eggs in their plastic wrap shells in advance, leave them to cool, and simply heat them up on demand, removing the plastic wrap when done.

This has changed my poaching life: I merrily make poached eggs almost every day now. No more fear of broken yolks or ectoplasmic whites. I am such a confident egg-poacher that I happily make Eggs Florentine for brunch for friends. Well, sort of. I draw the line at making hollandaise at weekends, so I have developed my own version, which has the happy result of being less calorific and super quick.

All you have to do then is toast your muffins and poach your eggs—which you could have prepared earlier but, really, how hard is it to poach eggs to order now that you have my special, failsafe method?

SERVES 4
1 box (10 oz [280 g]) frozen leaf
  spinach (not chopped)
¼ cup [60 ml] vegetable stock
¼ cup [60 ml] light cream
Salt and freshly ground black
  pepper
4 to 8 eggs (depending on
  hunger and greed)
Oil, for greasing (optional)
4 English muffins
1 tsp butter
Snipped chives, to serve
  (optional)

METHOD

Place the spinach in a saucepan, pour over the vegetable stock, and simmer until the spinach has defrosted. Beat in the light cream, and season with salt and black pepper to taste.

Put a pan of water on to boil.

Line a ramekin with a very large square of plastic wrap, overlapping the edges. (If you are nervous, a drop of oil in the bottom will help ease off the plastic wrap when the eggs are cooked.)

Break an egg into the ramekin and pull up the edges of the plastic wrap to form a money bag. Twist the top to seal. Repeat with each egg.

Lower the money bags carefully into the water, and cook for 3 minutes for runny middles, or 5 minutes for "œufs mollets," where the yolk is semi-cooked.

Halve and toast the muffins, and butter as liberally as you dare.

Cut the top of each egg moneybag with a pair of scissors, and carefully peel off its plastic wrap jacket. Discard.

Dollop some spinach mixture on each plate, add 2 muffin halves, and place an egg on top. A sprinkle of chives is good.

THE PERFECT BURGER

There are as many methods for a perfect hamburger as there are chefs on this planet. After sampling many, many burgers in my kitchen, I came to the conclusion that less is more every time. So, there are no crumbled crackers, no bread crumbs, no Worcestershire sauce, or chili seasonings in the LLG burger. It's simply pure ground beef with a finely chopped shallot, flavored with parsley for some pep.

You can make them as regular burgers or down-size and make sliders; those little two-mouthful patties that are so popular as appetizers.

We like to go traditional with our toppings, so I just add a slice of tomato, some red onion rings, a little crunchy lettuce—about the only time we find iceberg acceptable—and, sometimes, some burger sauce made from ketchup and mayo mixed together. Maybe the odd gherkin if we are in the mood.

MAKES 4 LARGE OR 6 MEDIUM BURGERS
1 shallot, finely chopped
1 tsp butter
1½ lb [750 g] ground beef
Handful flat-leaf parsley leaves,
 chopped
Salt and freshly ground black pepper
4 to 6 burger buns
Burger Sauce (see page 31), optional
4 to 6 thick slices of tomato
4 to 6 leaves of crunchy lettuce, e.g., iceberg
1 red onion, cut into rings

METHOD
Gently cook the shallot in a little butter until translucent.

Mix together the shallot, ground meat, parsley, and plenty of salt and black pepper, and shape into patties with your hands. Put in the fridge for 30 minutes.

Heat up a nonstick frying pan or griddle, and slap your burger in. Cook for about 3 minutes on each side if you like them pink within, 4 for well done.

Slice the burger buns in half, spread over the Burger Sauce, if using, and sandwich with a patty, a slice of tomato, a lettuce leaf, and some onion rings.

1. MUSHROOM AND HALLOUMI BURGER

While I like a good bean burger, not a lot can beat the simple combination of a grilled flat mushroom, a thick slab of halloumi, a slice of tomato, and some crisp lettuce leaves for the required chew. This is perfect for a weekend lunch, or for a kitchen supper with friends.

SERVES 1
1 large flat mushroom
Olive oil, for frying
Salt and freshly ground black pepper
1 thick slice of halloumi or Queso Para Freir cheese

For the burger sauce
1 tsp mayonnaise
1 tsp tomato ketchup
1 tsp Dijon mustard

METHOD
Fry the mushroom in a generous splash of olive oil over low heat in a small frying pan, with a lid over the top, for about 5 to 10 minutes. Season with salt and black pepper.

If cooking several mushrooms for several burgers, it is worth preheating the oven to 350°F [180°C], putting the mushrooms in an ovenproof dish, drizzling olive oil over them, top and bottom, and stretching foil tightly over the dish. Roast them for 15 to 20 minutes.

Put a frying or griddle pan over medium heat, and when hot, add the halloumi. Cook for 2 minutes each side, or until lighly browned and pliable.

Mix together the burger sauce ingredients. Sandwich the halloumi and mushroom in a roll spread with the burger sauce. The best accompaniments are pesto, tomato, and lettuce.

Eat. With plenty of napkins.

2. CORN FRITTER BURGER

I have yet to meet anyone, including fussy children, who does not like these. Best of all, they are extremely easy and quick to make. I particularly like them sandwiched in a roll, but they are just as good for breakfast with a poached egg, or for lunch with raita and a salad.

SERVES 4
¾ cup [100 g] all-purpose flour
½ cup [50 g] chickpea flour
1 tsp baking powder
Large pinch of salt
1 grind black pepper
2 generous pinches of paprika (optional)
2 eggs
²/₃ cup [150 ml] milk
1½ cups [280 g] corn kernels
Small handful flat-leaf parsley or cilantro leaves, very finely chopped (optional)
1 Tbsp vegetable oil, per 2 fritters

METHOD
Sift the flours and baking powder into a large bowl. Add the salt, pepper, and paprika, if using. Beat the eggs together with the milk, and add slowly to the flour, constantly beating to form a smooth batter. Add the corn, and the parsley or cilantro.

Set a large frying pan over medium-high heat, adding 1 Tbsp vegetable oil. Once hot, add 2 Tbsp mixture to the pan for each fritter. (Cook 2 at a time.) Smooth the mixture out, and after about 2 minutes, when the edges are bubbling, flip over to cook the other side. (The top should still be wet when flipped.) Press down on the cooked top side with a spatula to ensure the inside of the fritter cooks, otherwise, you will end up with a crispy outside and raw middle. Check the underside, and if necessary, flip again until crisp on each side.

Remove from the pan to a plate lined with paper towels. It's best served with caramelized onions, yogurt, and lettuce in a soft roll (I like 2 per roll).

3. GLAMORGAN BURGER

The only connection that Glamorgan sausages have to their piggy counterparts is their shape: instead of being stuffed with pork, the main ingredients in these traditional Welsh sausages are Caerphilly cheese (a hard cheese, also from Wales), leeks, and bread crumbs.

It's a delicious combination, which also makes a fine vegetarian burger, slapped between bread and laced with tomato ketchup. I've added some dried red chili flakes to mine, but that's entirely optional.

SERVES 5 TO 6

2 medium leeks
1 tsp butter
3½ cups [200 g] fresh bread crumbs, plus an extra 1¾ cups [100 g], for the crisp coating
1 heaping cup [100 g] grated Caerphilly cheese (a hard cheese like Monterey Jack or cheddar can be subbed)
Salt and freshly ground black pepper
½ tsp mustard powder
1 tsp dried chili flakes (optional)
1 Tbsp chopped flat-leaf parsley
3 eggs
Generous ¼ cup [65 ml] milk
Approx. 4 Tbsp oil, for frying

METHOD

Cut the dark green parts off the leeks, discard, and shred the whites finely by quartering lengthwise, and then cutting each quarter lengthwise again into fine strips. Cut these strips into 2-in [5-cm] sections.

Heat the butter in a frying pan, and when melted, add the leeks. Cook gently over medium heat until the leeks are soft. They must not brown, and will take about 10 minutes. When cooked, remove to a plate so that they can cool quickly.

Place all the dry ingredients in a large mixing bowl (bread crumbs, grated cheese, salt, pepper, mustard powder, and chili flakes, if using) and mix together with your hands to ensure everything is distributed evenly. Then add the cooled, cooked leeks and chopped parsley and mix again.

Beat together 2 of the eggs in a separate bowl, and then add to the dry ingredients. Mix together and then form into 5 to 6 hamburger-shaped patties.

Beat the last egg in a bowl with the milk. Pour the rest of the bread crumbs into a lipped baking pan. Take a patty and place it gently in the egg mixture, then lift it out using a spatula, allowing any excess egg to drip off. Then place the patty in the bread crumbs and flip over so it is completely covered. Make sure that the sides are breadcrumbed, too. Repeat until all the patties are coated.

Heat 2 Tbsp oil in a heavy frying pan, and cook the patties, 2 at a time, over medium heat, pressing down gently to ensure the patty makes contact evenly with the base of the pan. Do not fry over too high a heat, but do make sure that they heat all the way through. They draw up quite a lot of oil, so if you prefer, bake these in a moderate oven instead. They will take about 25 minutes to warm through, and a quick flash under the broiler will ensure a crisp finish.

I like to use a crisp white roll to contrast with the burger's soft middle. Cut it in half and layer up with cream cheese, spinach, and chutney.

4. CAULIFLOWER AND QUINOA BURGER (GLUTEN-FREE)

Cauliflower cakes are a perfect standby for those days when you want to roll out of bed towards the stove: you can make them the night before and, as a bonus, they are less likely to fall apart in the frying pan after a few hours in the fridge. They make an excellent morning-after-the-night-before brunch, packed as they are with vitamins and good things. Note that you will need a food processor to make cauliflower rubble in this recipe. Don't forget to use gluten-free bread rolls if serving to celiacs.

If you can find red quinoa, then a combination of half-red and half-white quinoa looks great.

MAKES 6 TO 8
1 cup [175 g] quinoa
1/2 head of cauliflower
  (9 oz [250 g]), cut into florets
White and green parts of
  4 scallions, chopped
Handful flat-leaf parsley or
  cilantro, finely chopped
2/3 cup [50 g] grated Parmesan
  cheese
Grated zest of 1 lemon
Salt and freshly ground black
  pepper
1 heaping cup [100 g] chickpea
  flour, plus extra for dusting
4 eggs, beaten together
Plenty of sunflower oil,
  for frying

METHOD
Cook the quinoa according to the package instructions, drain, and leave to cool. Roughly chop the cauliflower and reduce to fine rubble in a food processor, using the pulse button.

Pour the cauliflower rubble into a large mixing bowl and add the chopped scallions, herbs, Parmesan, and lemon zest. Generously season with salt and black pepper. Sift in the chickpea flour and mix it all together with your hands.

Add the cooled quinoa to the mixture and mix again. Pour over the beaten eggs and really thoroughly combine. You will end up with a very, very wet mixture, but do not be disheartened. The egg is necessary to bind the mixture: as it cooks, the proteins solidify, and stop the cake falling apart.

Pour a generous amount of flour onto a dinner or shallow soup plate. Take a handful of the wet mixture, form into a patty in your hands and place in the flour. Very gently lift and turn it over, so that both sides are thickly covered in flour.

Place a large frying pan over medium-high heat, and add 1 Tbsp oil. When it is smoking, slide your first 2 patties into the oil. Do not be tempted to cook more than 2 at a time, as they will lower the temperature of the oil. Press down gently with the back of a spatula.

Flip over very carefully after about 2 to 3 minutes to cook the other sides. You may need to flip again to ensure an even browning. When cooked, remove to a plate lined with paper towels. Each pair takes about 4 minutes to cook.

These are wonderful with a poached egg on top, with a fresh tomato chutney; but best of all I like them sandwiched in a bread roll with some red onion, guacamole, and cherry tomatoes.

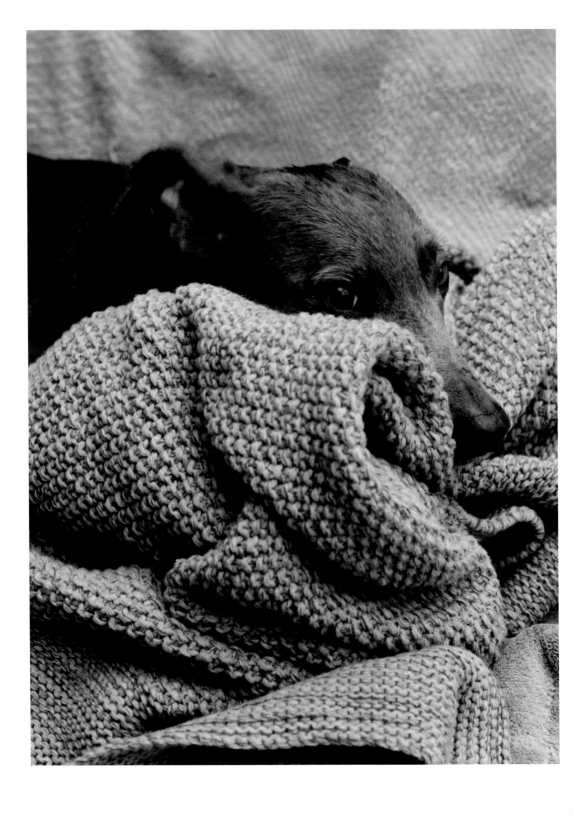

FOOD TO EAT WHEN YOU COME IN FROM THE COLD

Sometimes I think that a large part of the pleasure in a long, winter walk is coming in from the cold, knowing that you have earned a delicious, rib-sticking treat of a meal. After all, anticipation always adds spice to the eating, and the exercise earns you a big plate of something carbohydrate-filled.

I think there is a particular kind of food that is perfect for eating when you are cold to the marrow; food that acts as central heating for the body, as well as for the soul. It's going to be hot, comforting, and possibly nostalgic, too.

What it won't be is complicated, cold, or time-consuming to prepare. Quite a few of these recipes can be made in advance and simply reheated when ravenous people return from the great outdoors.

A word from the wise: never undercater and remember the phrase, "hungry as a hunter."

SASHA'S HANGOVER CURE: FRIED GNOCCHI WITH MOZZARELLA AND CHERRY TOMATOES

This is the most popular recipe that I have ever written; a fact that still slightly bemuses me. It is particularly indulgent, and very addictive. So maybe it's just the combination of salty, buttery, crispy, carby goodness, with the umami hit of the tomatoes that does it?

SERVES 2 GREEDY PEOPLE
1 package vacuum-packed gnocchi
1 Tbsp olive oil
2 Tbsp [25 g] butter
A few handfuls cherry tomatoes, halved
1 ball mozzarella cheese
Handful basil leaves
Salt and freshly ground black pepper

METHOD
Simply boil a large pan of salted water, add the gnocchi, and cook according to the package instructions (a few minutes).

Fish out when cooked and drain. Meanwhile, heat the olive oil and butter in a large, nonstick frying pan.

When the oil is hot, add the gnocchi (be careful, the oil will spit) and the tomatoes.

After about 5 minutes, when the gnocchi have started to catch and brown, add in ripped-up pieces of the mozzarella.

The temptation is to keep stirring, but you want the gnocchi to stick so that their bottoms go all crispy, so resist the temptation to keep prodding them. And if you mix it up too much, the cheese will melt into a lump of goo. (If that does happen, just use some kitchen scissors to cut it up.)

Tear the basil leaves over everything and season with salt and black pepper. Then eat. Lots.

WINTER WARMING DRINKS

A CLASSIC HOT TODDY
Into a heatproof glass, place a spoonful of honey, a squeeze of lemon, and a shot of whiskey. Top up with boiling water, and stir (with a cinnamon stick, if you feel so moved).

INFUSED HOT APPLE JUICE
Place the zest from one orange, a teaspoon of brown sugar, and three or four cloves in a saucepan and heat with 3¼ cups [750 ml] apple juice (cloudy is nicest).

INDULGENT HOT CHOCOLATE WITH MARSHMALLOWS
Heat 1 quart [1L] whole milk to a simmer, divide 1 cup [150 g] dark chocolate chips (60 to 70 percent cocoa solids) between four mugs and pour over the hot milk. Stir until melted and top with marshmallows.

CAULIFLOWER-CHEESE SOUP

Rich, creamy, intensely savory, velvet-textured: this soup is, frankly, a hug in a mug. It's also a great way to get some vegetables into children. (My godchildren love it.)

SERVES 4 TO 6

1 Tbsp vegetable oil (peanut or sunflower are good)

1 medium onion, chopped

1 very large head of cauliflower (approx. 2¼ lb [1 kg])

4½ to 6½ cups [1 to 1.5 L] vegetable or chicken stock

2 tsp Dijon mustard

Heaping 2 cups [200 g] grated Monterey Jack or cheddar cheese

Salt and freshly ground black pepper

1 Tbsp chopped flat-leaf parsley

Blender

METHOD

Find a big saucepan, pour in the oil, turn the heat to medium, and throw in the onion.

Reduce the heat to medium-low—the onion should cook slowly, without browning. Push the bits of onion around in a desultory way with a spatula from time to time, to check that they aren't sticking. This will take about 15 minutes.

In between prodding the onion, chop up the cauliflower into small pieces (removing the stalk and outer leaves), and when the onion is translucently soft, throw the cauliflower rubble into the pan.

Then you need about 4½ cups of stock. (It's going to depend on the volume of your pan compared with the cauliflower—the liquid should just cover the pieces.) Heat the stock in a separate pan, and then pour it over the cauliflower.

Cook the cauliflower until it is soft. This will take about 10 minutes.

Use either a stick blender or goblet blender to whizz the cauliflower to a soup consistency. If using a goblet blender, return the soup to the pan. Add the mustard and the grated Monterey Jack, and stir until it is all melted.

Check the consistency of the soup. If it looks too thin, bubble it up on the stove to reduce the liquid; equally, if too thick, add a little more stock/hot water.

Season generously to taste with lots of black pepper and salt. I sometimes add a little chopped flat-leaf parsley, or a splash of truffle oil.

CHICKEN, ORZO, AND PARSLEY SOUP

Chicken goes particularly well with orzo, the tiny rice-shaped pasta, as neither overwhelms the other. That being said, this soup is full of flavor, enhanced by a splash of chili sauce, and a squeeze of lemon at the end. I like it because you can prepare the main part hours in advance, leaving only the final hotting up to do when you crash through the door, desperate for something warm to eat. That's because the labor can be divided by poaching the chicken well in advance, stripping the meat off the bone, and then leaving both the stock and the meat in the fridge until 10 minutes before you want to eat it, which is all the time you need to cook the pasta in the stock.

SERVES 4

1 lb [500 g] chicken portions
¾ cup [100 g] orzo
Large handful flat-leaf parsley leaves, chopped
1½ lemons
Chili sauce (optional); I use either Sriracha, or chili oil

SECRET

I use two drumsticks and two thighs for this recipe, but you could use breasts. Do make sure the meat is on the bone, however, as you want the goodness for the stock.

METHOD

Rinse the chicken portions under the cold faucet and place in a saucepan. Cover the portions with cold water, bring to a boil, cover, and reduce the heat so that the water simmers. Cook for 45 minutes. (The chicken will be cooked after about 25, if you are in a hurry, but I like a richer stock, which comes from the longer cooking time.)

Using tongs or a slotted spoon, transfer the chicken to a cutting board to cool. Using fingers, discard the skin and remove the chicken from the bone. If it is breast, shred the meat into strips; if legs or thighs, tear into small pieces, discarding pieces of cartilage and any fatty bits.

Pour the cooking liquid through a sieve into a large measuring cup, being careful to leave the cooking scum behind on the bottom of the pan. Make up the stock with hot water to 3¼ cups [750 ml], pour into a clean saucepan, and bring to a boil. Add the orzo and cook until al dente. This will take around 5 to 6 minutes.

Add the chicken, three-quarters of the chopped parsley, and a squeeze from the half lemon. Stir through the soup. Ladle out into bowls and sprinkle the remaining parsley leaves on the top. Quarter the remaining lemon. Serve with chili sauce and the lemon quarters within easy reach.

WINTER-WARMING BEEF, BARLEY, MUSHROOM, AND CARROT STEW

One-pot meals like stews really are a wonderful thing to come home to after a long walk in the countryside, or poking around in the garden.

If you add lots of vegetables and barley, then you will also have a very robust, nutritious, and comforting meal. One of the best things about a stew like this is that once you master the basics, then you can vary the ingredients with different meats, vegetables, and herbs. If you don't want to use wine, you can replace this with more stock (either make this from scratch or use stock powder).

SERVES 4 TO 6

3 large carrots
2 celery stalks
1 large leek
1 large onion
1 garlic clove
3 cups [250 g] chopped crimini mushrooms
3 Tbsp olive oil, plus 2 tsp
1½ lb [750 g] stewing steak, cut into chunks
½ cup [100 g] barley
1 cup [200 ml] red wine
3 cups [750 ml] stock of your choice
A couple of sprigs of thyme
2 bay leaves
Salt and freshly ground black pepper

SECRET

This is a spectacularly good one-pot recipe that will stand you in good stead time and time again. The leftovers will happily reheat, so it's worth making a hefty batch to see you through those can't-cook/won't-cook evenings.

METHOD

Peel and chop the carrots and celery into small pieces. Slice the leek into ½-in [1-cm] rounds and then halve them. Chop the onion and the garlic together. Cut the mushrooms into sixths and reserve separately from the other vegetables.

Place a flameproof casserole dish on the stove over medium-high heat, add 2 Tbsp olive oil, and fry the beef in batches until browned all over. This will take about 15 to 20 minutes. Be careful not to overcrowd the pan as the meat will braise, not brown.

Remove the beef to a deep plate. Replace the casserole dish on the stove, add another tablespoon of oil, heat, then add the onion, leek and garlic. Fry for about 15 minutes over medium-low heat until the onion is soft. (Once you add liquid, the onions will stop softening, so it is important to take your time over this stage.)

Add the barley, stirring it through the onion, and cook for a few minutes.

Then add all the other vegetables, apart from the mushrooms, and fry with the onion for a couple of minutes. Put the beef back in the pot with the vegetables, and pour over the wine and the stock. Add the herbs. Cover with a lid and cook over low heat for about 1½ hours.

Fry the mushrooms in 2 tsp olive oil until soft, then add to the stew. Cook the stew for another 30 minutes.

Check the seasoning toward the end, and add salt and black pepper to taste. Serve with either mashed potato, or wide, flat noodles, such as pappardelle.

PORK, CHORIZO, AND LIMA BEAN STEW

Tomato-y, intensely savory, meaty, filling: this is one of those hero dishes that your friends and family will ask you to cook again and again. What you don't need to tell them is how uncomplicated it is to produce, and very pleasingly, just how inexpensive it is too. A couple of pounds of outdoor-reared boneless pork shoulder will usually cost around $10, and this dish will feed six comfortably.

METHOD

Choose a pan that is large enough to eventually cook your stew—I use a sauteuse, a wide, shallow cross between a straight-sided frying pan and saucepan.

Pour a couple of tablespoons of oil into the pan over medium heat, add the pork pieces in batches, and fry for 10 minutes, or until browned on the outside, but not completely cooked through, then remove from the pan.

Add the chorizo to the same pan, and fry for about 3 to 4 minutes. Remove it from the pan and set aside with the pork.

Add the onion to the same pan, and sweat over medium-low heat for 10 minutes, until soft and translucent. Don't be tempted to hurry them: burnt onions are not nice. Add the garlic and cook for 2 to 3 minutes.

Pour in the wine and water, and bring the mixture to a boil. Simmer for a few minutes before adding the sugar, chopped tomatoes, tomato paste, and lima beans. Add the pork and chorizo. Bring the mixture to a gentle simmer over low heat, place a lid over the pan, and cook for 1 hour. Keep checking it to make sure that it doesn't catch, and add a little more water if the stew looks like it is becoming too dry.

Just before serving, check the seasoning, and add salt and pepper to taste. I like to serve this in wide shallow bowls, sprinkled with the parsley, and over a big pile of mashed potato with buttered spring greens or kale on the side.

SERVES 6
Olive oil, for frying
2 lb [1 kg] boneless pork
  shoulder, cubed
1½ cups [250 g] chopped
  chorizo
1 large onion, chopped
2 garlic cloves, finely chopped
1 cup [200 ml] white wine
¾ cup [200 ml] water
1 Tbsp sugar
28 oz [800 g] canned chopped
  tomatoes
Squirt of tomato paste
1¼ cups [200 g] canned lima
  beans, rinsed and drained
Salt and freshly ground black
  pepper
4 Tbsp chopped flat-leaf
  parsley

PUFFED-UP BREAD BAKE WITH CHEESE AND HAM

In the UK, this would be called a "pudding" but do not be alarmed. It is merely that bread cooked in a savory custard is traditionally referred to as a pudding, for reasons long lost. What this is, is a dish of bread cubes, cut from a white loaf—never pre-sliced—steeped in a mixture of milk and beaten egg, which causes it to rise beautifully in the oven. (It is a kissing cousin to my Hot Cross Bun Bread-and-Butter Pudding on page 137). The cheese gives it a delectably crisp and crunchy topping, which contrasts with the fluffy, light interior.

The ham can either be slices torn into strips or, better still, cubes from a chunk of meat.

You can serve this as a hearty one-dish supper, accompanied by a green salad with a sharp dressing to cut the richness, or use it as the starch to accompany a stew or a roast. It's also a clever dish to have up your sleeve as a winter vegetarian meal—omitting the ham, of course.

SERVES 6 AS AN ENTREE OR 8 AS A SIDE DISH

2½ cups [250 g] grated Monterey Jack or cheddar cheese (see Method)
2 eggs
1¾ cups [400 ml] milk
Salt and freshly ground black pepper
Butter, for greasing
5½ cups [275 g] cubed white bread (no crusts)
⅔ cup [100 g] ham, torn

SECRET

This isn't something you should cook in advance because it flops as it cools, making it look a lot less appealing.

METHOD

Preheat the oven to 350°F [180°C].

If you are grating the cheese in a food processor, use the smallest grating disk, as this helps the cheese melt more evenly and go even further.

Beat together the eggs and milk, adding a grind of black pepper and a pinch of salt (not too much because of the salty cheese), then add two-thirds of the cheese.

Butter a gratin dish liberally—this will give crisp, browned sides to your pudding—and arrange the bread cubes in it. They should be tumbled, as opposed to laid out in serried ranks, so that the top of the pudding is uneven. Sprinkle the ham over and between the bread cubes.

Pour over the egg mixture, making sure each bread cube is doused in the liquid. Then liberally scatter over the rest of the Monterey Jack cheese.

Bake in the oven for 25 to 30 minutes, but resist the temptation to open the door during cooking, as this will cause the bake to deflate. It's ready when the top has browned, and the bake has puffed up. Serve immediately.

CHICKEN AND ROOT VEG TAGINE

I first made this Moroccan-inspired stew when I was snowed in with my mother a few years ago. We had woken up to find everything blanketed in virginal white. The snow kept coming down and the gritters hadn't been to our tiny village, so lunch was whatever I could come up with from the pantry.

In weather like that, all I want to do is eat delicious, spicy food—central heating for my soul. I found some chicken thighs in the freezer; and sweet potatoes, a butternut squash, and an aging potato in the cupboard. I gathered up some olives and some blanched almonds, which ended up absorbing some of the lovely cooking juices, and adding a great textural contrast to the meltingly soft vegetables. Served over some couscous, mixed with the seeds of a pomegranate that was lurking in the crisper drawer, it was the perfect winter lunch. Ten minutes' prep; forty minutes' bubbling with an occasional stir.

SERVES 6

6 chicken thighs with skin on
  (about 2¼ lb [1 kg])
Flour, for dredging
2 Tbsp olive oil
1 onion, finely chopped
1 Tbsp Moroccan spice (I use
  ras-el-hanout or Berbere
  spice blend)
½ tsp ground cinnamon
1 medium sweet potato,
  cut into large chunks
1½ cups [200 g] peeled and
  cubed butternut squash
1 lb [500 g] white potatoes,
  peeled and cut into large
  chunks
1 heaping cup [150 g] blanched
  almonds
1 heaping cup black and/or
  green olives (in my view, you
  can't have too many almonds
  or olives in a tagine, so add as
  many as you like)
1⅔ cups [400 ml] water
1 Tbsp finely chopped
  preserved lemon, if possible
Couscous with pomegranate
  seeds and slivered almonds,
  to serve
Chopped herbs, to garnish

METHOD

Rinse the chicken thighs under the faucet and pat dry with paper towels. Pour some flour into a shallow, wide bowl, and dredge the chicken through it.

Heat the olive oil over high heat in the wide frying pan in which the tagine will eventually be cooked. When the oil is popping, brown the chicken, 3 pieces at a time. (If added all at the same time, it will reduce the cooking temperature of the oil, making the chicken soggy.) You are not cooking the chicken through, just browning it properly on all sides. This will take about 20 minutes. Once brown, remove the pan from the heat and place the chicken pieces on paper towels to drain.

When all the chicken has been browned, leave the fat in the pan, lower the heat to medium, add the chopped onion, and cook slowly until it is translucent (about 10 minutes).

When the onion is cooked, add the Moroccan spices and cinnamon, and stir the onion over the heat for 1 minute. Add the chicken pieces and ensure they are covered in the onion spice mixture. Add all the chopped vegetables, along with the almonds and olives.

Add the water and simmer for about 40 minutes until thickened and rich. Some of the potato chunks will break down, which will help to thicken the sauce. Add the preserved lemon, if using, 5 minutes before the end of the cooking time.

Serve with couscous. If you feel like it, add the pretty seeds of a pomegranate and some slivered almonds. Garnish the tagine and couscous with chopped fresh green herbs.

MINI MACARONI AND CHEESE

We ate a lot of mac and cheese as children and I think it is now hard-wired into my brain as the ultimate comfort food. While we often had variations—maybe roast beef leftovers chopped on Monday and layered over the pasta, or some buttery, fried bread crumbs added to the cheese topping—it is the simple version to which I always return, seduced as I am by the silken, smooth sauce; powerful

cheese hit and tummy-filling goodness.

I've never really understood the approach that sees the traditional béchamel replaced by a mixture of cheeses—even, God forbid, cottage cheese. Use too much cheese and the mixture goes grainy, often separating to leave a film of orange oil on top of the pasta.

My special ingredient is Dijon mustard: the kick enhances the cheese flavor beautifully without it tasting, well, mustardy, and it helps thicken the sauce, too. I also find that it slightly lessens the amount of cheese that you need to use, as it adds so much rich flavor.

On that note, be careful not to over-thicken the sauce before you add the pasta, as the macaroni will absorb some of the liquid when it is flashed under the broiler and you will end up with "gluey" mac and cheese—the cardinal sin.

SERVES 6 (IT IS VERY RICH)
2½ cups [250 g] grated Monterey
   Jack or cheddar cheese, plus
   1½ cups [150 g] for the topping
3½ cups [350 g] macaroni
3 Tbsp [45 g] butter
⅓ cup + 1 Tbsp [50 g]
   all-purpose flour
4½ cups [1 L] whole milk
3 Tbsp Dijon mustard

UTTERLY ADDICTIVE EUROPEAN CHEESE

Keen's farmhouse cheddar *is a classic rich unpasteurized Cheddar from Somerset in southwest England that is wonderful served as a big chunk surrounded by grapes and chutneys.*

Delicious crumbly unpasteurized **Pouligny-St-Pierre** *is an "appellation d'origine contrôlée" triangular goat cheese that looks great on a cheese board. It's the local cheese where I spend my summer holidays in France, and I've learned to look for the green label packages—these are the "fermier" (farmhouse) cheeses, as opposed to the red ("industriel").*

If I want to serve a single cheese, then I often choose the **Waterloo** *from Berkshire. It's mild, semi-soft, with a buttery flavor and made using a wash curd method.*

Its distinctive yellow color is due to the natural carotene in the unpasteurized milk, which comes from a single herd of pedigree Guernsey cows near Henley.

If you love Brie, then it's worth seeking out the less common **Brie de Melun**. *It has a lovely, almost rippled-looking darker rind in contrast to the paler Brie de Meaux, and an almost salty tang to the creamy interior. Make friends with your local cheese shop so it's at the perfect point (not too runny) when you come to serve it.*

I have a thing for very creamy French cheese, and one of my all-time favorites is **Saint-Félicien**. *A small-ish round, soft cheese, it's intensely rich, with a soft bloom to the rind. I often serve one of these alone for the cheese course if I'm just having three or four people for supper.*

METHOD

Keep the grated cheese for the sauce and topping separate. I use the grating attachment on my food processor, but it can equally well be done by hand. (I keep bags of grated odds and ends of cheese in the freezer, and add them straight to the sauce without defrosting.)

Cook the macaroni in plenty of boiling water, according to the package instructions—usually about 8 minutes. After the macaroni is drained, pour over a kettle of boiling water to rinse off some of the starch, as this helps reduce the risk of unpleasant starchiness.

Meanwhile, melt the butter until it sizzles, and sift in the flour—do sift, as it helps avoid lumps. Stir together rapidly, until a smooth paste is achieved. Then, start to add the milk. I like to start with about ²/₃ cup [150 ml], just to get the sauce going. When that is mixed together, add another cupful [250 ml] and whisk this together, being sure to scrape the corners of the pan, where the paste congregates. When it has started to thicken, add another big slosh of milk and vigorously whisk together.

Add the mustard, which you will find helps the thickening process, and whisk.

Continue until all the milk has been added. (I like to add the milk in increments as I find it thickens more quickly this way, and there is less likelihood of the sauce catching.)

Add the 2½ cups [250 g] grated cheese and beat into the sauce with a wooden spoon.

Turn on the broiler to medium-high.

When the sauce is thick, but still slightly runny, add the macaroni and stir carefully together.

You can either spoon this into one big dish, or in individual ones. I find it fills about 6 small pots.

Strew the grated cheese for the topping over the macaroni. Place under the broiler for about 5 to 10 minutes, until the top is golden and bubbling. Do keep an eye on it, as it can burn in an instant.

Serve with a green salad or some sliced tomatoes.

GRATED POTATO GRATIN

This is very good hot as an entrée (leave out the ham for an excellent vegetarian option), served with a green salad. It also works well as a substantial side dish, served with roast chicken or pork chops, and is equally good cold as hot—we used to take chunks of it in our school lunchboxes. It reheats like a dream, both in the oven and microwave.

The recipe is adapted from the 1971 cookbook, *Poor Cook*, by Caroline Conran and Susan Campbell, from which much of my mother's kitchen repertoire came. It is one of the first things I learned to cook, and was a foolproof standby that served me well all through university in Newcastle where, in winter, an icy wind whips over the city from the North Sea, and food that can be used as internal central heating is essential.

SERVES 6 AS AN ENTREE OR 8 AS A SIDE DISH

1 Tbsp softened butter, plus extra for greasing and topping
1 lb [500 g] potatoes
1 Tbsp olive oil
½ large onion, chopped
1 garlic clove, crushed
2 slices [50 g] ham, cut into thin strips about 1 in [2.5 cm] long (optional)
2 eggs
⅓ cup [25 g] grated Parmesan cheese
1 cup [100 g] grated Gruyère or Monterey Jack cheese
1¼ cups [275 ml] whole milk
Couple grinds of black pepper
Pinch of grated nutmeg

> ### SECRET
> The best potatoes for this dish are waxy potatoes such as Yukon Gold.

METHOD

Preheat the oven to 350°F [180°C]. Use a piece of paper towel and a little butter to grease a gratin dish.

Peel the potatoes and grate them. This can be done with a box grater, but it is the work of moments (and runs less risk of grating your fingertips) if you use the grating attachment on a food processor, which I highly recommend.

Put the grated potatoes into a bowl, and then squeeze out all the starchy liquid with your hands over the kitchen sink. However, it is important not to rinse the potatoes at any point, as you need some starch to thicken the dish. (You will be amazed at how much liquid comes off the potatoes.)

Add the olive oil and butter to a frying pan over medium-low heat, and when the butter has melted, fry the onion and garlic for about 10 minutes, being careful not to brown then. Add the ham, if using.

In a large mixing bowl, beat together the eggs, Parmesan, half the Gruyère or Monterey Jack, plus the milk, black pepper, and nutmeg.

Add the cooked onions to the grated potatoes, and mix together. Spoon everything into the buttered gratin dish, then pour over the eggy cheese mixture. Flatten the top of the potatoes and dot the top with the butter. Strew the remaining grated cheese over the dish.

Bake in the oven for approximately 45 minutes. Depending on the depth of the dish, and heat of the oven, this can take from 35 to 60 minutes, so do keep an eye on it. If the top is browning too quickly, loosely cover it with a piece of foil.

GRANNY HORSE'S CROSS-HATCHED POTATOES

This dish has always been known as Granny Horse's Potatoes: I've never seen potatoes cooked in this way elsewhere, and every time I eat them, I am transported back to her tiny cottage, filled with equestrian memorabilia, in the beautiful village of Avon Bassett in Warwickshire, England. That's Granny Horse in the photo on the right.

My grandparents had the luxury of a huge garden. Granny ended up in charge of the flowers, and Grandpa was very much in charge of vegetables, which he grouped in serried ranks. Peas, beans, lettuces, leeks, parsnips, cabbages, and, of course, potatoes, all made their way straight from the soil to the kitchen.

This way of cooking potatoes, which Granny showed me, really pays homage to the taste of a great potato, because they are good enough to eat on their own. The edges caramelize in the heat of the oven, and they are simultaneously fluffy, crispy, and chewy. Please don't be scared by the amount of butter: think about the amount you'd put on a baked potato. Do not substitute margarine or oil, as the potatoes will not crisp.

SERVES 4 (I USUALLY COUNT
ON 3 HALVES PER PERSON)
6 large potatoes
11 Tbsp [150 g] butter, softened
Salt and freshly ground black
  pepper

METHOD
Preheat the oven to 350°F [180°C]. Halve the potatoes lengthwise and score them about ½ in [1.2 cm] deep, in a criss-cross pattern, with three strokes in each direction. Spread butter thickly over the surface—the liquid content of the potatoes can make the butter slide, but persevere. Sprinkle a generous amount of salt and black pepper over each half, and bake for about 45 minutes until golden and cooked through.

> ### SECRET
> A floury potato is what's best here—it really doesn't work with new or waxy potatoes, so I recommend Russet or generic Idaho baking potatoes.

SALADS AND FOOD FOR HOT SUMMER DAYS

Salads are, hands down, the most popular recipes that I write on my blog. Usually they are a result of pulling out whatever is lurking in the fridge and adding whatever fresh fruit and veg looked good at the store that day. I think it's that ease that appeals: most of them take minutes to assemble, yet feel like so much more than the sum of their parts.

I always think it's cheating a bit to call a salad a "recipe," when mostly it's just a case of combining a few ingredients; this means that the secret of a successful dish is in the things you choose to mix together. A good rule of thumb is always to include a protein (cheese, legumes, meat) and a fruit (tomato, avocado, cucumber, pomegranate seeds), with something leafy, and maybe some seeds or nuts.

I also think it's important not to be worried about measures or finding the exact same ingredients. A little more or less of anything rarely hurts a salad, and often substitutions can be inspired. That being said, it's probably best not to play around too much with the proportions of a salad dressing, as the mixture of flavors is usually calibrated with thought.

If you have room, it's worth collecting some interesting oils and vinegars and playing around with dressing ideas. I have walnut oil, hazelnut oil, avocado oil, and an excellent cold-pressed canola oil; plus a proper, aged, and sticky balsamic vinegar, white wine vinegar, and sherry vinegar. Good mustards are also a great way to perk up a salad. Try wholegrain, or one that is infused with herbs or spices.

LIBERTYLONDONGIRL'S SALAD

This is one of the most popular recipes I have ever written. I must admit to a slight astonishment, given its simplicity, but then again, it is the salad that I eat all year around with a few variations, and I reckon it comes in at under 15 minutes from fridge to mouth. It's wonderful in winter, because the crunch of the onion and the sharp tang of the lemon juice con your senses into believing that spring could be just around the corner.

Best of all, it has just four main ingredients. Of course, you could substitute pretty much any kind of cheese for the halloumi, but do think about the contrast of textures. A vegan reader once asked about substituting marinated tofu in this recipe, and I don't see why not, as long as it is firm or pressed tofu.

Do not make this salad in advance, as the avocado goes mushy.

SERVES 4

1 red onion
1 avocado
1 cup [240 g] canned chickpeas, rinsed and drained
Good squeeze of fresh lemon juice
Lemon zest (optional)
½ lb [250 g] halloumi or Queso Para Freir cheese
Salt and freshly ground black pepper
Dash of good olive oil (preferably the herby, grassy Greek stuff)
1 Tbsp chopped flat-leaf parsley
Lettuce leaves and toasted pita bread, to serve

METHOD

Finely chop the red onion by making vertical slices, and then cutting crosswise before chopping some more.

Roughly dice the flesh of the avocado and mix it with the chickpeas and onion, adding the lemon juice and some zest, if you like. Hands are good for this.

Cut the halloumi into slices about ¼ in [0.5 cm] thick, then place in a hot frying pan (a griddle pan if you have one) without any oil, until it is browned on each side. Chop it up into small bite-sized pieces. (I always cook more than I need for the salad as I tend to eat quite a lot en route …)

Add the halloumi to the rest of the ingredients, along with salt, black pepper, the olive oil, and parsley. Mix together well.

Serve with lettuce leaves (Romaine or Little Gem, if you happen to find it in the farmers' market), and pita bread, for scooping.

GREEN LENTILS AND GOAT CHEESE WITH MUSTARD DRESSING

I used to make this for lunch for my roommate, Jackie, and me on those summer days in Manhattan's East Village when the heat seemed to shiver in the air above the sidewalk, and spending any time at all in our un-airconditioned apartment kitchen felt like a trial. Sitting on the tiny fire escape, eating this from mismatched, chipped bowls, five floors up from the street, we watched New Yorkers briskly walking down the block, seemingly unaffected by the heat.

The creamy cheese, earthy lentils, peppery watercress, and piquant mustard really are one of those great salad combinations.

SERVES 4 FOR LUNCH
OR 6 FOR A FIRST COURSE
1¼ cups [250 g] Puy or green
   lentils
1 cup [150 g] quinoa
½ cup [125 g] cubed or
   crumbled goat cheese (I like
   the kind that comes in a fat,
   round slice with a cloudy
   white rind)
1 Tbsp chopped flat-leaf parsley
Salt and freshly ground black
   pepper
Generous handful watercress
1 romaine lettuce, chopped

For the dressing
1 tsp Dijon mustard
1 Tbsp olive oil
Dash of lemon juice or
   balsamic vinegar

METHOD
Put 2 saucepans of water on to boil.

Cook the lentils and quinoa separately in lots of simmering water according to the package instructions. While they are cooking, make the dressing. Put the mustard, olive oil, and lemon juice or balsamic vinegar in a bowl, and whisk well (or put in a jar and shake).

When the lentils and quinoa are cooked, drain them, and rinse briefly in cold water to remove the starch and cooking scum. Add to a large bowl with the dressing, and mix in. Add the goat cheese and parsley, and season with salt and black pepper. Serve with the watercress and lettuce.

BUFFALO MOZZARELLA WITH BLOOD ORANGES

In cold, dark January, when the nights seem longer than the days, eating delicious blood oranges gives a promise of summer ahead. Streaked with dark red in both flesh and peel, they give a subtle hint of raspberry along with their citrus tang.

In this salad, they make a delicious contrast to the salty olives and cheese, and everything is balanced by the crisp lettuce.

You do need to remove the pith and membrane from the orange pieces, but learning to supreme an orange is a very handy skill, although you may destroy a few before you get the knack. First take a very sharp, small knife and slice off the top and bottom of the fruit, taking care not to cut too deep. Then slice all the peel, pith, and membrane from the fruit, top to bottom, revealing the fruit underneath. Slip the knife along each vertical segment to remove each slice with no pith or membrane attached.

SERVES 4 AS AN APPETIZER
2 buffalo mozzarella cheeses
2 blood oranges
1 romaine lettuce
½ cup [50 g] black olives, pitted
Olive oil
Salt and freshly ground black
  pepper

METHOD
Drain the mozzarella and pat dry with paper towels. Then tear the mozzarella into small pieces. (Do not cut it.)

Supreme the oranges (see introduction, above) and pull each supreme of orange in half.

Remove the outer leaves of the lettuce and discard (or make the Lettuce Soup on page 103). Slice the lettuce crosswise into ½-in [1-cm] pieces.

Cut the olives in half lengthwise.

Divide the ingredients between 4 plates, and drizzle over a little olive oil. Season with salt and black pepper.

Orange-Scented Fragrances for a Perpetual Summer

I always wear a citrus fragrance—preferably one with orange blossom notes—and these are some of the tried-and-tested favorites that I always have in my home.

Fragonard Fleur d'Oranger Eau de Toilette

Diptyque Fresh Lotion for the Body

Le Labo Neroli 36 Perfume Oil

Tom Ford Neroli Portofino Eau de Parfum

Jo Malone Orange Blossom Cologne

Malin+Goetz Neroli Candle

Molton Brown Orange & Bergamot Body Wash

SOBA, PEANUT, AND TOFU SALAD

Although this is Japanese in origin, it always reminds me of St Mawes in Cornwall (in the far southwest England), where my friend, Hannah, first made it for our lunch when we were on vacation one summer. I was unenthusiastic at the prospect, but she had control of the stove and I do try not to take over every kitchen into which I walk ... At the first mouthful I felt rather stupid, as it was a revelation. I never thought cold noodles could taste this good: the crunch of the pepper with the sharpness of the dressing, the yielding quality of the tofu, and the slippery noodles make this a strangely addictive dish.

SERVES 4

8-oz or 9-oz package [200 g]
  soba noodles
1 carrot
Bunch scallions
1 red bell pepper
Half a 14-oz package [200 g]
  firm tofu
Handful cilantro or mint
  leaves, finely chopped

For the dressing

^{2}/$_3$ cup [125 g] crunchy peanut
  butter
Handful roasted unsalted
  peanuts, finely chopped
1 Tbsp rice vinegar
Juice of ^{1}/$_2$ lime
1 garlic clove, crushed
^{1}/$_2$-in [1-cm] piece ginger, grated
1 Tbsp honey or agave nectar
2 Tbsp soy sauce

METHOD

Cook the noodles according to the package instructions, then refresh in cold water. Drain well.

Grate the carrot and slice the scallions, pepper, and tofu in slivers or matchsticks.

Combine all the dressing ingredients in a large bowl, and add all the chopped vegetables and the tofu. Then carefully toss in the noodles and herbs, ensuring they are all covered in dressing.

STYLISH AND DELICIOUS PLACES TO REST YOUR FEET IN DEPARTMENT STORES

BG IN BERGDORF GOODMAN (NEW YORK)

On the seventh floor of Bergdorf Goodman, this pale-blue sanctuary designed by cult decorator Kelly Wearstler, with its ravishing view over Central Park is the spiritual home of Manhattan ladies-who-lunch. But, fear not, there is more than salad and tuna tartare to eat here: the lobster mac 'n' cheese is artery-sticking-ly good and the croque monsieur a gourmand's delight.

5th Avenue at 58th Street, New York NY 10019;
www.bergdorfgoodman.com

ROSE BAKERY AT DOVER STREET MARKET (LONDON, NEW YORK, AND TOKYO)

Paris's lovely Rose Bakery has expanded internationally under the aegis of possibly the world's most directional fashion superstore with its cult assiette de légumes, and delicious baked goods (the carrot cake is particularly noteworthy), providing a down-to-earth counterpoint to the often extraordinary clothes on sale next door. Warning: they often sell out of savory food before 4 P.M., so do arrive early.

www.doverstreetmarket.com

PRIMO PIANO AT LE BON MARCHÉ (PARIS)

On the Left Bank in Saint-Germain-des-Prés, the venerable Bon Marché hides a wonderful secret—Primo Piano, with its adjacent outdoor, tree-shaded courtyard serving good Italian food, as well as tartines and a killer cheesecake.

Le Bon Marché, 24 Rue de Sèvres, 75007 Paris;
www.primo-piano.fr

THREE BRILLIANT BOOKSTORES FOR COOKS IN NEW YORK

1. JOANNE HENDRICKS

Not far from my old Manhattan apartment, this wonderful bookstore also sells all manner of culinary ephemera, including menus, prints, photographs, cookware, and etiquette guides, in addition to a glorious assortment of rare food books. If you are looking for a particular first edition, this is the place to ask.

488 Greenwich Street, New York, NY 10013; www.joannehendrickscookbooks.com

2. STRAND BOOKSTORE

Because the Strand buys thousands of books every day, including secondhand, and has the largest rare books collection in New York City, they have a phenomenal cookbook department, with plenty of treasures by long-forgotten cookbook writers to be unearthed. They also have great discounts on list prices (often cheaper than Amazon).

828 Broadway, New York, NY 10003–4805; www.strandbooks.com

3. KITCHEN ARTS & LETTERS

With over 13,000 titles in stock (domestic and imported, contemporary and out of print), this not-very-big store in the upper reaches of the Upper East Side has an influence far beyond its size. Do sign up to its brilliant newsletters.

1435 Lexington Avenue, New York, NY 10128; www.kitchenartsandletters.com

AND ONE IN LONDON ...

BOOKS FOR COOKS

This Notting Hill-based store is legendary amongst UK food lovers. Their café tests recipes from the cookbooks, and cookery classes take place in the demonstration kitchen upstairs. I also highly recommend curling up in their delightfully squashy sofa to test-read the books.

4 Blenheim Crescent, Notting Hill, London W11 1NN; www.booksforcooks.com

KALE WITH WALNUT DRESSING

Whenever I am in Los Angeles, it can seem as though no one there eats anything but kale. Steamed, raw, chipped: it is on every menu. And with good reason. Kale is a superfood, packed with nutrients. Don't be put off by serving it raw: just make sure you chop it very fine to minimize the necessary chewing.

SERVES 4
½ cup [50 g] walnuts
2 Tbsp walnut oil
1 tsp sherry vinegar
3 Tbsp natural yogurt
Salt and freshly ground black pepper
½ lb [250 g] kale

METHOD
Roughly chop the walnuts and place in a frying pan over medium-high heat for about 5 minutes, until they are lightly toasted.

Set aside 1 Tbsp walnuts and place the remainder in a food processor with all the other ingredients, except for the kale. Pulse until the nuts are quite small. Taste, and season to your liking. (This is quite a sharp dressing, but it does work very well against the kale.)

Run a sharp knife down each side of the kale stems to remove them, then roll each leaf half into a sausage, and slice very thinly. This will give fine strips of kale.

Heap the kale into a serving dish, pour over the dressing, and mix through. Sprinkle over the reserved, chopped walnuts.

CUCUMBER AND SESAME SALAD

This is a simple and refreshing salad that clears the palate. Perfect on a hot summer day. (See photograph on page 61.)

SERVES 4 AS A SIDE DISH
1 cucumber
2 Tbsp white sesame seeds

For the vinaigrette
1 Tbsp peanut oil
2 tsp sesame oil
2 tsp rice vinegar
2 tsp mirin or Chinese rice wine
Pinch of superfine sugar

METHOD
Peel the cucumber and slice it thinly, either with a very sharp knife, or using a mandoline on its middle setting.

Arrange the cucumber on a serving dish. Whisk together the vinaigrette ingredients and pour over the cucumber. Scatter the sesame seeds over the top just before serving.

AVOCADO, GRAPEFRUIT, AND RED ONION SALAD

This is a salad that divides opinion, but I think the creaminess of the avocado and the crunch and tang of the onion, paired with the sharp, citrus hit of the grapefruit, is a wonderful combination.

I first made it in New Jersey with a big, fat, Florida pink grapefruit and a couple of perfect avocados I had bought in Delicious Orchards, one of my favorite NJ fresh produce markets. (I love it for the name, as much as anything).

As well as a quick, light lunch, this is a perfect first course, too, as it gets the taste buds going.

SERVES 4
1 large pink grapefruit
1 red onion
2 avocados
1 round, soft lettuce (such as Butterhead)

For the dressing
Squeeze of lime juice
2 Tbsp good olive oil
1 tsp Dijon mustard (optional)
Salt and freshly ground black pepper

METHOD
To supreme the grapefruit, using a very sharp knife, slice the peel and pith off the grapefruit (see page 55) and release the segments from the tough membranes. I don't like big segments in my salads, as I find them too overpowering—better to break them up if they are very big. For the same reason, slice across the red onion into rings as fine as you can get them. Then halve them.

Peel and slice the avocados as thinly as possible, then cut each slice into pieces. Roughly chop the lettuce and put in a serving bowl then arrange the avocados, grapefruit, and onion on top.

Combine all the ingredients for the dressing (I like to shake them together in a jam jar) and drizzle over the salad.

GRILLED ZUCCHINI WITH LICKABLE DRESSING

Every day in the middle of the annual August zucchini glut, I see pleas on Twitter from English people wanting recipes to use them up, before they bolt and end up with rhino-thick skin. My two favorite ways to cook them are either grated and stir-fried, then mixed into pasta or noodles, or grilled—as they are here.

I vary this salad with different dressings, but I made this simple yogurt one for my oldest schoolfriend, Clare, one night, and I caught her licking her plate, so it has fans other than me.

SERVES 1
1 zucchini
Olive oil

For the dressing
4 tsp natural yogurt
Salt and freshly ground black pepper
3 mint sprigs, leaves finely chopped

METHOD
Chop the zucchini lengthwise into thick slices. Slick them with olive oil and place into a preheated, ridged, cast-iron grill pan on top of the stove. Resisting the temptation to keep prodding them, leave them for about 3 to 4 minutes each side, before turning them onto a plate.

For the dressing, thin the yogurt with water to a pouring consistency and season with salt and black pepper. Pour onto the zucchinis and top with the mint.

To go with this, I usually make a salad with soft lettuce leaves: a romaine; skinned cucumber chunks; a handful of chopped, green beans zapped in a puddle of water in the microwave for 2 minutes and refreshed under the cold faucet; and a couple of celery stalks, chopped.

Over it all, I sprinkle some good olive oil and sometimes pumpkin, sunflower, and sesame seeds.

MIDWINTER SALAD WITH ROASTED CAULIFLOWER, MAPLE WALNUTS, AND POMEGRANATE

This is for a wintry day when you despair of ever having a full day of sunlight. The sweet-sour flavors and the crunch of the seeds and walnuts make this quite addictive. (I first made it for a dinner party I threw at my London apartment for a group of fashion editors, and they inhaled it.)

There are quite a few processes to get through in this salad, but it helps that they can all be done in advance (even the night before), although I do think that the cauliflower is much nicer roasted just before you need it, so that it is pleasantly warm in the salad, rather than cold.

SERVES 6 TO 8
1 large head of cauliflower
2 Tbsp olive oil
Salt and freshly ground black
  pepper
1 Tbsp maple syrup
1 Tbsp light brown sugar
¾ cup [75 g] walnuts, very
  roughly chopped
½ pomegranate
Couple handfuls watercress

For the dressing
2 Tbsp tahini (sesame paste)
½ Tbsp pomegranate molasses
2 Tbsp olive oil
Generous pinch of salt
2 tsp fresh lemon juice

METHOD
Preheat the oven to 400°F [200° C].

Divide the cauliflower into florets and then break into smaller pieces. Put in a roasting pan and toss with the olive oil and some salt and pepper. Roast for about 30 minutes, until the cauliflower is browned—almost charred—in places.

In a small bowl, mix together the maple syrup and brown sugar, and add the walnuts. Mix with your hands, then transfer to a nonstick frying pan over high heat and toast for about 10 minutes, stirring frequently, until they caramelize. Keep an eye on them so that they do not catch and burn.

Hold the pomegranate half over a bowl and bash the back with a wooden spoon. Miraculously the seeds will pop out. Pick over them, removing any bits of white pith.

Make the dressing by mixing together all the ingredients.

Place some watercress on each plate and then divide the cauliflower, pomegranate seeds, and walnuts between each one. Drizzle over the dressing using a spoon.

FASHION MUSEUMS I LOVE

UK: Fashion Museum at Bath Assembly Rooms
Every year a guest curator picks a dress of the year. They are all on display, and make a wonderful cultural history of fashion dating back to 1963. There is also a lovely selection of dressing-up costumes for children.

Bennett Street, Bath, Somerset BA1 2QH; www.nationaltrust.org.uk/bath-assembly-rooms

UK: Fashion Collection at the V&A, London
Spanning four centuries, the V&A's Fashion Collection is the largest and most comprehensive collection of dress in the world. (I'm pleased to note that my aunt has a pair of shoes in there.) Do keep an eye out for the regular special exhibitions.

Cromwell Road, London SW7 2RL: www.vam.ac.uk

UK: Dress and Fashion Collection at The Museum of London
I love wandering around the Galleries of Modern London here, as the clothes are displayed contextually, so you can see their cultural relevance. There are around 60 complete outfits and more than 200 accessories dating from the late sixteenth century to the present day.

150 London Wall, London EC2Y 5HN; www.museumoflondon.org.uk

UK: The Fan Museum, Greenwich, London
The fan museum—in two grade II-listed houses built in 1721, within the Greenwich World Heritage Site—is home to more than 4,000 predominantly antique fans from around the world, dating from the eleventh century to the present day. As a bonus, it has a wonderful tea room.

12 Crooms Hill, London SE10 8ER; www.thefanmuseum.org.uk

UK: Gallery of Costume at Manchester Art Gallery
The Gallery of Costume is housed in the elegant Platt Hall, an eighteenth-century textile merchant's home, and contains over 20,000 items from the seventeenth century to the present day.

Platt Hall, Rusholme, Manchester M14 5LL; www.manchestergalleries.org

France: Les Arts Décoratifs, Paris
Part of the Louvre buildings, Les Arts Décoratifs is actually four collections, amongst which is Mode et Textile. While the permanent collection here is for scholars, the temporary exhibitions it puts on—from the history of underwear to a Hussein Chalayan retrospective—are always fascinating, beautiful, and make a welcome break from the lure of the Parisian stores.

107 Rue de Rivoli, 75001 Paris; www.lesartsdecoratifs.fr

US: The Museum at FIT (Fashion Institute of Technology), New York
I would spend hours here when I lived in New York: quite apart from its spectacular temporary shows, the Fashion and Textile History Gallery changes its exhibits very six months, pulling pieces from its permanent collection of over 50,000 garments and accessories from the eighteenth century to the present day.

227 West 27th St, New York, NY 10001: www.fitnyc.edu

US: Costume Institute at the Metropolitan Museum of Art, New York
Its yearly fashion exhibition grabs headlines worldwide, thanks to Anna Wintour's ceaseless championing of its cause and, while some of the previous concepts seem a little tenuous (Superheroes: Fashion and Fantasy springs to mind), shows like the recent Alexander McQueen Savage Beauty were unmissable.

1000 Fifth Avenue, New York, New York 10028-0198; www.metmuseum.org

HALLOUMI AND PERSIMMON SALAD

My very first memory of persimmons is seeing them on a large, flat tray in long-closed Greek-Cypriot restaurant, Milou's Kebab House, on Charlotte Street in London's Fitzrovia—a place I was first brought to in my carrycot. I must have been around seven or eight, and I remember asking my mother what they could possibly be. They are bright orange, sized somewhere between a plum and a nectarine, with the smooth, slightly shiny skin of both, but with a coronet (known as the pistil) of leaves on top. Sliced into, they are fleshy with no visible seeds. Taste-wise, they are very, very sweet.

In recent years, they've become much more common. Every time I see them, I get to thinking about salt and sweet together—a taste combination I've only ever liked in retro cheese-and-pineapple sticks. I wondered what would happen with very salty halloumi cheese (or Queso Para Freir if you can't find halloumi) against the super-sweet persimmons. I now know that it works brilliantly: I added a trickle of reduced balsamic vinegar and the acid enhanced the salt-sweet combination perfectly.

This would make a wonderful Christmas Day appetizer. The combination of taste bud-accelerating ingredients would be perfect before the creamy, carby richness of the entrée. (You can slice the cheese in advance, and reduce the balsamic, but do not slice the persimmons before you need them, as they will brown and go woolly.)

There are no precise quantities for this. Allow one persimmon per person, sliced across, not down, so that you get a pretty star effect in the middle of each slice; and use the same number and width of halloumi slices. Heat the cheese in a hot griddle pan (with no oil), if you have one—a frying pan will do—until it is browned on each side.

Pour a few tablespoons of balsamic vinegar into a saucepan and heat gently until reduced to a thick syrup. (It only takes a minute or two, so keep an eye on it, otherwise it sticks like glue to the pan.)

Then layer the pretty orange persimmon and cream-colored cheese slices together. Sprinkle over kosher salt and some black pepper. You could serve it with watercress or a little bit of chopped mint, but it's just as good served plain, on its own.

KOHLRABI REMOULADE (SORT OF)

This is my modern play on a traditional remoulade dressing, which is most often a mustard-flavored mayonnaise, usually seen in France coating grated, raw celery root.

I only started eating kohlrabi last year: I had seen the pastel-green and slightly shiny bulbs, with their alien tentacles, on my local market stall, but had no idea what to do with them. It didn't help either that my dear French friend, Yoann, refers to them as "food for ze cattle."

When one arrived in my weekly farm vegetable box, looking like it had just landed from a sci-fi props store, I stared at it for a while, then sliced a bit off. And blow me down if it didn't taste, not like the earthy root I was expecting, but rather like a raw broccoli stalk. Delicious. I didn't want to cook it, so I thought that a riff on the creamy remoulade dressing would complement that green, fresh crunch. You can make this a little in advance as the lemon juice stops the kohlrabi discoloring.

Do try it: it's now one of my favorite quick salads.

SERVES 6 AS A SIDE SALAD

2 lb [1 kg] kohlrabi (about 5 small bulbs)
2 tsp Sriracha chili sauce (add more if you like a kick)
6 Tbsp mayonnaise
2 tsp lemon juice
Salt and freshly ground black pepper

METHOD

Peel off the outside of each kohlrabi with a vegetable peeler and lop off the tentacles with a paring knife.

Grate the kohlrabi using either a box grater or the standard grating attachment on a food processor. (Do be careful not to use the ultrafine grating attachment as this makes the kohrabi too fine and watery.)

Mix the chili sauce into the mayonnaise, along with the lemon juice. Add the kohlrabi and mix through the dressing.

Taste and season with salt and black pepper.

GRILLED BELL PEPPERS WITH PRESERVED LEMON, PINE NUTS, AND MINT

Inspired both by a trip I took to Marrakesh with my sister, and by one of my mother's failsafe appetizers, this classic dish of bell peppers is perked up by the salty mouth-pucker of the lemons, while the mint adds a lovely, fresh note.

SERVES 4

8 red, sweet, pointed Romano
  bell peppers
3 Tbsp pine nuts
2 Tbsp good olive oil
1 preserved lemon, to taste
3 large sprigs of mint, leaves
  roughly chopped, plus extra
  whole leaves to garnish
Salt and freshly ground black
  pepper
Pita bread, olives, radishes,
  and capers, to serve

METHOD

Preheat the broiler to high, then place the bell peppers on a rack and broil for 7 to 10 minutes, until they are blistered and blackened. Turn them over with tongs and broil the undersides, too. Put the peppers in a large, plastic food bag, seal, and set aside for 10 minutes—this makes the skins easier to remove.

Meanwhile, toast the pine nuts in a frying pan until golden. Transfer to a plate and set aside.

Remove the skins and stalks from the peppers and discard both, then cut the peppers in half lengthwise, and remove the seeds and membrane. Cut the peppers into long strips, and transfer to a large bowl, along with any cooking juices from the bag. Pour over the olive oil.

Halve and seed the preserved lemon, finely slice, then add to the bowl of peppers along with the chopped mint leaves. Season with salt and black pepper. Set aside for an hour or two, allowing the flavors to mix.

To serve, remove the peppers and lemons from the bowl using tongs and arrange on a serving platter. Pour over the oil from the marinade, sprinkle with the toasted pine nuts, and garnish with the whole mint leaves. Serve with warm pita bread and little dishes of olives, radishes, and capers.

ROASTED CHERRY TOMATO AND CORN SALAD

I always adored succotash when I lived in America. Before I landed, I'd read about it in novels, but really had no idea what it actually was until I was fed it at Thanksgiving one year. For those of you who also have no idea, it's a dish of stewed corn kernels and lima beans, cooked with chopped tomatoes and onions, served warm. That was the inspiration for this dish. There are no lima beans and no stewing, but the basic premise of delicious fresh corn and tomatoes remains the same.

SERVES 6 AS A SIDE DISH

2 lb [1 kg] cherry tomatoes
Decent drizzle of Greek olive oil
Sprinkling of coarse salt
Lots of black pepper
Fresh, torn basil
4 corn cobs or 1 cup [250 g]
  canned corn kernels

METHOD

Preheat the oven to 300°F [150°C].

Place the tomatoes, olive oil, salt, black pepper, and some torn basil in a roasting pan and put in the oven to roast.

While they are cooking, slice the corn kernels vertically off the cob using a sharp knife. (I learned to do this in New Jersey: it's not a usual way of preparing corn in the UK, where it's pretty much always served on the cob, or bought in kernels either sold in a can or frozen.)

Roast the tomatoes for about 30 to 40 minutes until really soft and slightly caramelized around the edges. They will give off lots of liquid. Leave the oven on.

If using canned corn, remove from the can, leaving behind the juices, and set aside. Pour into the roasting pan with the tomatoes and return to the oven for about 15 minutes so that the flavors can mingle, and the corn soften a little.

Pour the tomatoes, corn, and juices into a serving bowl, and add more basil to serve.

SECRET

If you can buy your corn cobs at a market, ask to taste the kernels. They should be sweet, plump, and fresh. If they are at all chewy, dry, or bland then used canned corn kernels.

KITCHEN SUPPERS

I've been lucky enough to have had a large dining table to fit my friends around in my London apartments, but when I lived in Manhattan, I had a tiny, galley kitchen and a doll's house-sized table. I didn't let that stop me from having people around to eat, though: four people squeezed at the table and me at the stove made for many happy evenings. (Not least because I was one of the very few people in my circle that ever cooked. That New York cliché about storing sweaters in ovens is a cliché for a reason.)

I just cannot imagine not cooking supper for my friends and family, wherever I find myself. Whether it's in my friend Julian's crazy band house in Los Angeles' Koreatown, where I served up late-night Indian meals to the boys after rehearsal; or in Ibiza after a long weekend of dancing, when it's all about outdoor feasts of restorative salads, gathering up everyone around a table for a relaxed meal is one of the loveliest ways to spend time with friends.

In London I cook supper at least twice a week for a motley crew: I invite whoever is around to join me and I cook simple meals that don't require me to stop work early, or spend hours chopping.

This chapter is the cumulative result of cooking for my friends around the world, with whatever came to hand at the time. There are recipes I've stolen from my mother—and grandmother. There are things I like to eat when I'm on my own (a kitchen supper can just as easily be for me and the sausage dog as for the five thousand), and dishes friends ask for again and again. Above all, they are uncomplicated and delicious.

MUSHROOM LASAGNE

There's very little I dislike more than a parsimonious vegetarian lasagne, redolent of school dinners, filled with lumps of watery vegetables, metallic tomato sauce, a white sauce that has been all but sucked up by the noodles, and topped with a few cheese scrapings. If you're going to bother with lasagne, it should be thick, luxurious, and wholly satisfying. There are three or four different versions in my arsenal, but my absolute favorite is this mushroom one, using lots of different types of mushroom. (There will be no watery zucchini, inappropriate root vegetables, unpleasantly soft eggplant, or insufficiently cooked-down tomatoes on my watch.)

SERVES 8

1 quantity Slow-Cooked Tomato Sauce (see page 82 and made using only chopped and cherry tomatoes)
3 lb [1.5 kg] mushrooms (I like portobello, white, and crimini)
4 Tbsp [50 g] butter
3 Tbsp olive oil
Approx. 10 to 14 lasagna noodles

For the cheese sauce
4 Tbsp [50 g] butter
1/3 cup + 1 Tbsp [50 g] all-purpose flour, sifted
2 cups [500 ml] whole milk
2 Tbsp Dijon mustard
2½ cups [250 g] finely grated Monterey Jack or cheddar cheese

For the topping
1½ cups [150 g] finely grated Monterey Jack or cheddar cheese
1⅓ cups [100 g] fried bread crumbs (to make your own, see method on page 75), or panko bread crumbs (optional)

METHOD

Make the Slow-Cooked Tomato Sauce first so that it is happily simmering away (for a minimum of 45 minutes) while you get on with the rest.

Slice the mushrooms into thirds, then across into cubes. Put a large frying pan over the heat with the butter and oil, and when the butter has melted, add the mushrooms. Don't let them cook too quickly: the trick is to soften the mushrooms without them losing their plumpness. When they are cooked, take them off the heat and set aside.

For the cheese sauce, melt the butter in a large, heavy-bottomed pan (this is to stop your sauce burning) and beat in the sifted flour.

Add a ladleful of milk and whisk in. As it thickens, carefully add in another measure of milk, and so on. Add in the mustard and the cheese, and beat together with a wooden spoon until the cheese melts. When the sauce has thickened enough so that it coats the back of a spoon without falling off, take it off the heat.

Preheat the oven to 350°F [180°C].

Pour a ladleful of cheese sauce over the entire bottom of a large gratin dish. Then add the first layer of lasagna noodles. (You may need to break some to ensure they fit neatly.)

Over this add a thin layer of tomato sauce. Then a layer of mushrooms, followed by a layer of cheese sauce. Next: a layer of lasagna. (Try to keep the layers as thin as possible.) Repeat until the dish is almost, but not quite, full. Make sure that the topmost layer is lasagna noodles spread with a little cheese sauce.

For the topping, strew over the cheese, then the fried bread crumbs, if using. Bake in the oven for about 35 to 45 minutes.

INDIVIDUAL CHICKEN POT PIES

Pie. **There's** a word to strike joy in the heart. Really, who doesn't like pie? There is rarely a situation where you can't serve a pie. I always serve Giant Chicken Pies at my annual birthday cocktail party (see page 173), and a fruit pie makes a perfect Sunday lunch dessert.

I also like little pies, which are great for supper parties. They are easier to maneuver and, if you are having a slightly smarter meal or, equally, one where there is already lots on the table with no room for a big dish, then everyone can be served a neat plate, with accompaniments. **The enamel dishes I use have a diameter of 4 in [10 cm] at the base and 5 in [12 cm] across the top**, but narrower and deeper dishes would work too.

These individual chicken and leek pot pies are one of my go-to recipes when I am having a work dinner at home. (I've yet to find a fashion editor who can resist these, pastry included.)

Ah, yes. The pastry. I make no apology for using ready-rolled all-butter puff pastry sheets in these little pies. Storebought pastry takes away all the stress, leaving you to concentrate on making the delicious, creamy middle.

Of course, I make the filling from scratch, which appeals to the thrifty side of my nature, as you will be left with lots of lovely chicken stock for soup afterwards.

MAKES 8 SMALL PIES

For the poached chicken
1 organic, free-range chicken, or 4 thighs and 4 leg pieces (2½ to 3½ lb [1.2 to 1.5 kg])
1 carrot
1 onion
1 leek

For the pies
7 Tbsp [100 g] butter, plus extra for frying
¾ cup [100 g] all-purpose flour, plus extra for dusting
1 Tbsp Dijon mustard
4½ cups [1 L] chicken stock (see Method)
2 leeks
Salt and freshly ground black pepper
2¼ lb [2 kg] ready-made puff pastry sheets
2 eggs, lightly beaten
8 mini pie dishes

METHOD

For the poached chicken, rinse the chicken under the cold faucet and place it in a deep saucepan. Roughly chop the vegetables and add to the pan. Cover the chicken with cold water, and bring to a boil.

Turn down the heat so the water stays on a gentle simmer, and poach the chicken for 1 hour. Test for doneness by pulling away a leg from the body to check for pinkness inside the thigh.

Remove the chicken from the stock to a board and leave to cool. Meanwhile, turn up the heat under the pan of stock, and allow it to bubble until it has reduced to 4 cups [1 L]. Set it aside.

Remove the skin from the chicken and discard, and then pick all the flesh from the carcass. Cut it into small pieces.

To make the white sauce for the pies, melt the butter in a large saucepan. When it is sizzling, add the flour. Stir around until you have a thick paste. Add the mustard and combine. Gradually pour in the reserved chicken stock, beating it into the paste with a wooden spoon. Allow to cook, stirring, until the sauce has thickened sufficiently.

Chop the white part of the leeks into thin rounds. Melt a small lump of butter in a frying pan and fry the leeks over medium heat until they are softened, but be careful not to let them burn or brown. Add them to the sauce and mix. Season with salt and black pepper.

Sprinkle flour over the work surface and lay out the puff pastry sheets. Place one pie dish upside down on the pastry as a template and cut 8 shapes that are ½ in [1 cm] wider than the dish all around.

Preheat the oven to 350°F [180°C].

Divide the chicken evenly between the pie dishes, making sure there is an even mixture of white and brown meat. Pour over the creamy leek sauce.

Using a pastry brush, paint one side of each pastry lid with the beaten eggs.

Take a piece of the cut pastry and carefully lower over a pie dish, egg side down. Then, take a fork and crimp the edge of the pastry all around to ensure it sticks. Using a sharp knife, trim the edge so there is no overhang. Brush the top of the pie with more of the beaten egg.

Bake in the oven for around 20 minutes until the tops have risen and are golden.

PANTRY ESSENTIALS

I don't think there's a cook alive who doesn't have a list of essentials on standby for impromptu dinners. I always have the obvious things (flour, sugar, spaghetti, pesto, potatoes, kosher salt), but there are a few others that can help you perform kitchen alchemy.

Pomegranate molasses to drizzle over halloumi and use in marinades and dressings.

Lemon juice in a bottle: better than a shriveled and moldy lemon in the fruit bowl.

Vegetable stock in powder form: I use it endlessly.

Chinese Shaoxing wine comes in a screw-top bottle, is best bought in Chinatown, but is now in many supermarkets. Wonderful in stir-fries and good for risottos and sauces in place of sherry.

Canned chickpeas are great to bulk out stews, add to curry sauces for last-minute vegetarian dishes, and whizz with olive oil for dips. Endless options, really.

Dijon mustard makes dressings and sauces taste so much better. Add a heaping tablespoon to lentils and goat cheese for a quick salad.

Miso powder added to boiling water and noodles or green vegetables gives you supper in five minutes.

TURKEY GRATIN

This is what we eat at my parents' house the day after Christmas. Always accompanied by a fluffy, butter-filled baked potato, this is a dish of leftover cooked turkey covered in a creamy, rich sauce made with stock, and thickened with a roux. The top is strewn with grated cheese, and over it all is a blanket of crisp, butter-fried bread crumbs. It is an intensely comforting dish.

Elizabeth David's version of the French classic *émincé de volaille* originally inspired this version, which is my mother's. There are two ways to make this: either with leftover meat or by poaching the turkey from scratch. If you do poach the turkey, you can then use the stock straight away in the sauce. (Of course this can be made with chicken, too.)

I like to serve this with kale or spinach to counteract the richness.

SERVES 6 TO 8 (IT IS VERY RICH)
1 lb [400 g] cooked turkey (if
poaching from scratch, you will
need 2 lb [1 kg] raw, bone-in pieces,
such as thighs)
2½ cups [600 ml] stock of your
choice
⅔ cup [150 ml] whole milk
5 Tbsp [65 g] butter, plus extra for
greasing
½ cup + 1 Tbsp [75 g] all-purpose
flour
1 Tbsp Dijon mustard
1 cup [100 g] finely grated cheddar
or Monterey Jack cheese
For the topping
1½ cups [150 g] finely grated
cheddar or Monterey Jack cheese
1¼ cups [100 g] fried bread crumbs
(to make your own, see Method
below), or panko bread crumbs

SECRET
If you are making the gratin in advance to serve the next day, top up the liquid to 4 cups [1 L] in total for the sauce, as it will thicken considerably overnight.

METHOD
Preheat the oven to 350°F [180°C].

Either chop the leftover meat and place in a buttered gratin dish, or poach 2 lb [1 kg] turkey thighs by covering them with water and simmering for approximately 30 minutes until the meat is cooked. Reserve the cooking liquid for the sauce, tear the meat from the bones, and place in the gratin dish, as above.

Mix together the stock and milk.

Meanwhile, melt the butter until it sizzles and sift in the flour—do sift, as it helps avoid lumps. Stir together rapidly, until a smooth paste is achieved. Then start to add the stock mixture. I like to start with about ⅔ cup [150 ml], just to get the sauce going. When that is mixed together, add about 1 cup more and whisk this together, being sure to scrape the corners of the pan where the paste congregates. When it has started to thicken, add another big slosh of stock and vigorously whisk together.

Add the mustard and continue stirring until all the liquid has been added.

Add the cheese and beat into the sauce with a wooden spoon.

When the sauce is thick but still slightly runny, pour over the meat in the gratin dish and stir carefully together.

For the topping, strew the grated cheese over the gratin, then the fried bread crumbs, and place in the oven for about 30 minutes, until the top is golden and bubbling. Do keep an eye on it, as it can burn in an instant.

TO MAKE YOUR OWN FRIED BREAD CRUMBS
Either use prepared fresh bread crumbs or make them yourself. Cut ½ lb [250 g] white bread, remove the crusts, and reduce to crumbs in the food processor, either with the blade or with the grating attachment: this will produce about 1¼ cups [100 g] crumbs.

Place 4 Tbsp [50 g] butter in a frying pan and when melted, add the bread crumbs and mix thoroughly. Keep an eye on them as they burn easily. They should take about 15 minutes to turn dark golden.

ZUCCHINI AND PEA ORZOTTO

Orzotto isn't made with orzo—the tiny, Italian pasta—but with pearl barley ("orzo" is the Italian word for barley). Pearl barley is a grain that holds up a lot better to liquid than risotto rice. The payoff is that you lose the unctuous creaminess of a risotto, but what you get in return is a lovely, resistant quality to the grain which, while still softened, holds its shape.

Orzotto has been a staple in my recipe head since I was a university student. It's cheap to buy and practically idiot-proof. That's because there's no great secret to producing a great orzotto. Unlike its kissing cousin, the risotto, it does not demand, or even need, dedicated wrist action or 45 minutes of close nurturing over the stove. You just add the hot liquid to the grains, mix it in, and simmer away, pausing every so often when you pass the stove to give it a stir and check it's not burning. It also cooks very quickly and you can be sitting down to eat in 30 minutes if you get moving.

SERVES 4

- 3 cups [750 ml] vegetable or chicken stock
- 1 Tbsp olive oil
- 1 onion, finely chopped
- 1 heaping cup [200 g] pearl barley
- 3 Tbsp [50 ml] white wine or pale sherry (Fino is delicious in this)
- 1 to 2 Tbsp butter
- ¾ of a zucchini [150 g], chopped into ½-inch [1-cm] slices, and then into cubes
- 1 heaping cup [150 g] frozen petite sweet peas
- ⅔ cup [50 g] grated Parmesan cheese
- Salt and freshly ground black pepper

METHOD

Heat the stock to a simmer.

Put a saucepan over medium heat and add the olive oil. When it is heated, add the chopped onion and cook gently until it is translucent—about 10 minutes. (Don't let it brown, as this will color the orzotto.)

When the onion has softened, add the barley grains and stir. Add the wine or sherry, and let it reduce by half.

Then add all the hot stock and simmer away for about 20 minutes until the barley is soft, but resistant.

While the barley is cooking, fry the zucchini cubes in the butter until soft, but not browned. Defrost the peas by pouring boiling water over them in a metal bowl or pan, then drain.

When the barley is cooked, add the grated Parmesan and the vegetables, reserving a few spoons of zucchini to put on top as a garnish. Stir everything together and add salt and pepper to taste.

SQUASH STUFFED WITH CREAMY MUSHROOMS

Stuffed bell peppers were the bane of my life as a teenage vegetarian: the practically raw shells, filled with a gluey, inedible mixture of barely cooked rice, with bullet-hard peas and bits of too-soft carrot, bound with egg. I swore I would never eat a stuffed vegetable as an adult.

I do love winter squash, though, and when I lived in New Jersey, there would be piles of squashes, gourds, and pumpkins in all shades of orange, yellow, cream, and green stacked up at roadside stands and in the pumpkin patches that proliferate along the highways.

So I thought a bit about what might go into that convenient hole that is left when all the seeds are scooped out, and decided that the answer might be mushrooms, bound in a light cream sauce. I find this works wonderfully.

SERVES 4

2 small, round squashes (like the striped ones)
1 Tbsp olive oil
2 Tbsp butter
2 cups [250 g] mushrooms, chopped small
1 garlic clove, crushed and chopped
2 sprigs of thyme, leaves removed from the stems
Salt and freshly ground black pepper
½ cup [100 ml] light cream

METHOD
Preheat the oven to 350°F [180°C].

Split each squash in half horizontally and scoop out the seeds. You will probably also need to level off the stem so that the top half can sit flat in the baking dish.

Brush each cut surface with oil, and place the squash halves, cut-side up, in an ovenproof dish.

Set a frying pan over medium heat and melt the butter until it fizzes. Add the mushrooms, garlic, thyme leaves, and a good pinch of salt and some black pepper. Cook slowly until the mushrooms are soft, then add the cream and bring to a simmer. You want the cream to thicken slightly, but not be runny. This should take about 5 minutes. The cream will thicken further on baking.

Scoop the mixture into the squash halves, cover tightly with foil, and bake for about 1 hour, depending on the size.

VEGETARIAN RESTAURANTS IN SINGAPORE THAT DON'T MAKE YOU MISS MEAT

WHOLE EARTH PERANAKAN-THAI-VEGETARIAN RESTAURANT

This fusion of Thai and Straits Chinese food is something you will only find in Singapore. There are lots of braised bean curd (tofu) and clever mushroom dishes, all bursting with flavor, and the emphasis is on clean food: no added MSG and no mock foods (no glutens, no fake chicken or fish).

76 Peck Seah Street, Singapore 079331; www.wholeearth.com.sg

GOKUL VEGETARIAN RESTAURANT, LITTLE INDIA

This may be a 21st-century take on an Indian restaurant, with Bouroullec-inspired plastic chairs, modern lampshades, and waiters in snazzy uniforms, but, nonetheless, the food is immediately recognizable, with delicious dosas, an epic vegetarian version of chicken rice, and very good murtabak.

19 Upper Dickson Road, Singapore 207478; www.gokulvegetarianrestaurant.com

LINGZHI

A very beige room and an unpromising location in an office building belies the extraordinary variety of food that appears on the menu here, with vegetables and mushrooms that will be new to a European palate. There is an emphasis on organic ingredients, and I always, always overorder because everything sounds—and tastes—so good.

Liat Towers #05-01, 541 Orchard Road, Singapore 238881; www.lingzhivegetarian.com

MUSHROOMS ON TOAST, THREE WAYS

For all the ways I know to cook mushrooms, there is something very pleasing about the simplicity of piling sautéed mushrooms onto a piece of perfect toast. I like, too, that not only can this be the ultimate indulgent supper for one, but also a delicious meal for friends gathered around the kitchen table. I particularly enjoy eating this in fall, when mushrooms are in season. It's scrumptious, heart-warming, and perfect for damp, foggy days.

I have lots of variations on this theme, but the key is making sure that all your ingredients are as fresh and as good as possible. With simple food, the flavors have really got to sing out, and skimping just makes the simplicity redundant.

Do choose good bread for this. Sourdough is excellent here, as is a close-crumbed rye, or a wholegrain seeded loaf.

The method is similar in all cases: prepare white, crimini, and portobello mushrooms by cutting them into thick slices and then slicing across to make cubes; tear oyster, Black Trumpet, or chanterelles into pieces. It's hard to be too generous when cooking mushrooms as they do cook down so much, but generally, I allow around 2 cups [250 g] mushrooms per head.

Add 3 to 4 tablespoons butter and a tablespoon olive oil to the pan, and when bubbling, toss in the mushrooms and cook gently until they are soft and give off their juices. Keep the heat on medium-low. You don't want the mushrooms to brown.

Season generously and spoon onto toasted bread. A squeeze of lemon is always good at the end.

I've offered some variations here; all recipes serve four.

WITH PARSLEY AND GARLIC

1 garlic clove, crushed
Very generous handful
  flat-leaf parsley leaves, chopped

METHOD
Add the garlic to the cooking mushrooms about 5 minutes in. Spoon the mushrooms over the toast, and strew with the parsley.

WITH WHITE BEANS, KALE, CHEESE, AND A BUTTERY SAUCE

1 cup [240 g] canned cannellini beans
2 handfuls kale, shredded (central stem removed)
4 Tbsp [50 g] butter
⅔ cup [50 g] grated hard cheese (Parmesan, Monterey Jack, or ricotta salata are all good)

METHOD
Add the beans, kale, and 1 Tbsp water to the nearly-cooked mushrooms. Clamp a lid over the pan for a few minutes until the kale is wilted. Throw in the butter and allow it to melt. Taste and season. Spoon the mixture over the toast, then grate some cheese over the top.

WITH MADEIRA CREAM

1 shallot or small onion, finely chopped
2 garlic cloves, finely chopped
¼ cup [50 ml] Madeira, sherry, or white wine
1 cup [250 ml] light cream
Fresh green herbs, if you have them
1 lb [500 g] spinach leaves

METHOD
Before you add the mushrooms to the frying pan, sweat the shallot or onion and garlic in the butter and olive oil over medium heat until translucent. Then toss in the mushrooms.

When they are softened, add the Madeira, sherry, or wine, turn the heat to high, and bubble it down for a few minutes to burn off the alcohol.

Turn the heat down to medium, add the cream, and stir around. Add the herbs, if using. Bubble for a few minutes while you rinse the spinach. Throw the wet spinach in a pan with the lid on (no extra water) and remove, once wilted (2 to 3 minutes), to a colander. Press out any extra water.

Check the seasoning of the mushrooms. If your sauce has bubbled down too much and is looking gloopy, add a bit of hot water to thin it out.

Divide the spinach over the toast and heap over the mushrooms and cream. Add a generous twist of black pepper.

BAKED CHICKEN THIGHS, THREE WAYS

I think we all have evenings where we optimistically invite friends around for supper, and then get stuck in the office, or on the phone, or on a bus that doesn't seem to move. Bolting into a supermarket an hour before my guests are due to arrive, because I have no time to prepare my planned meal, often results in my standing there like a rabbit in headlights, wondering if cheese is ever an acceptable supper option (well, yes; but also, no).

In this situation I often cook chicken thighs. They are one of those seemingly boring cuts of meat that undergo a magical transformation when shoved in a hot oven with aromatic herbs and lots of butter and oil. The darker meat is juicy, full of flavor, and the skin crisps up beautifully. There are also lots of bones to gnaw: I always think getting down and dirty with your food is the sign of a good kitchen supper amongst friends.

I always allow two thighs per person, and then several over. (So much nicer to be able to offer seconds, rather than attempting portion control.) Before cooking them, I usually turn them over and use scissors to trim off some of the skin that is tucked under, to allow the meat to cook evenly on the bottom.

Couscous, bulgur wheat, or quinoa goes very well with chicken.

SECRET
Please do buy free-range chicken: not only it is a Good Thing to do, those legs work a lot harder and consequently the meat tastes much better.

BASIC RECIPE

SERVES 4

10 chicken thighs

4 Tbsp [50 g] softened butter (zap in microwave for 20 seconds if necessary)

2 Tbsp olive oil

Salt and freshly ground black pepper

METHOD

Preheat the oven to 350°F [180°C].

Place the chicken thighs in a roasting pan or baking dish. Rub the butter into the thighs and drizzle with the oil. Liberally salt and pepper the chicken.

Bake for 45 minutes, or until cooked through.

WITH GNOCCHI, LEMON, AND ROSEMARY

4 to 5 sprigs of rosemary

1 package vacuum-packed gnocchi

Grated zest and juice from ½ lemon

METHOD

Follow the basic recipe, adding the rosemary to the baking dish with the chicken.

While the chicken is cooking, poach the gnocchi according to the package instructions.

When the chicken is done, remove to a plate to rest. Increase the oven temperature to 400°F [200°C], and add the gnocchi to the juices in the chicken dish. Bake for 10 minutes, or until the gnocchi is browned.

Remove the dish from the oven, and return the chicken to it. Add the lemon zest and juice. Serve at the table.

WITH PASTA AND GREEN HERBS

4 cups [400 g] dried pasta: penne or macaroni

2 generous handfuls mixed chopped, soft green herbs: try chervil, tarragon, thyme, parsley

METHOD

Cook the chicken following the basic recipe. Fifteen minutes from the end of the cooking time, cook the pasta according to the package instructions and drain, reserving a cup of the cooking water for later.

When the chicken is done, scatter over the herbs and serve with the pasta. Add the reserved pasta water to the baking dish, scraping up all the good bits from the bottom, and spoon the juices over the chicken.

WITH OLIVES, LEMONS, AND OREGANO

Generous handful fresh oregano, leaves finely chopped

5 lemons

1 cup mixed green and black olives, pitted

1 Tbsp chopped flat-leaf parsley

METHOD

Reserve 1 Tbsp oregano, then mix the rest with the softened butter and apply to the chicken thighs, following the basic recipe.

Quarter 4 of the lemons and add to the chicken dish before it goes in the oven.

Zest the final lemon.

Fifteen minutes before the chicken comes out, add the olives to the baking dish.

When the dish is finally removed, scatter over the lemon zest, parsley, and remaining oregano.

SLOW-COOKED TOMATO SAUCE

This sauce is one of my bedrock recipes. It's delicious on its own, but it also forms the base of so much that I like to cook—and eat. Once a month or so I cook up a huge vat of the stuff, freezing it into two-person portions, so there is always something to eat in the house without resorting to takeout menus or frozen dinners. (Don't be tempted to freeze large containers-full, even if you are a big family—they take forever to defrost. It's much better to freeze in small portions.)

I was taught to make this by my mother, and I've been cooking vats of it since I was in my early teens. The ingredients are things I think most of us would be able to find in the most basic of pantries.

The most important thing about this sauce is that you should cook it for at least 1 hour, and add a little sugar to counteract the metallic taste of the canned tomatoes. I just do not understand the countless recipes out there that call for canned tomatoes, and then require only 20 minutes' cooking time. All that can possibly give is a raw, harsh flavor. I like quite a lot of onion in my sauce, both for depth of flavor and for texture—it makes the sauce thicker.

SERVES 4 AS A PASTA SAUCE

2 Tbsp olive oil
1 large onion, chopped
2 garlic cloves, crushed (optional)
3 x 14.5-oz [400-g] cans tomatoes (my optimal combination is 1 can of whole tomatoes, 1 of chopped tomatoes and 1 of cherry tomatoes)
1 Tbsp tomato paste
1 tsp sugar
Salt and freshly ground black pepper

SECRET
Don't worry about using expensive branded canned tomatoes, or any other hand-plucked-by-organic-virgins-in-Italy ones, either. Whatever is cheap on the shelf at the supermarket will do fine.

METHOD

Put a nice big saucepan (I prefer wider to higher, as it cooks down more quickly) over medium-high heat, and add the olive oil.

When it's hot, toss in the onion, turn the heat right down, and sweat (i.e., slow-cook in oil) until translucent, pushing it around from time to time. This takes at least 20 minutes. Cook the onion too hot and fast and it will brown and caramelize. You want the onion to be soft and colorless. (You want it nice and soft because once it hits the tomatoes it won't get any softer.) Add the garlic, if using, 5 minutes before the onion is done.

Then pour in the tomatoes and tomato paste, and sugar. Heat it to simmering point (slow bubbling), then turn the heat to medium-low and simmer away, uncovered.

Do keep stirring regularly as the sauce has a nasty habit of sticking; turn down the heat if you think it is boiling too fast. I also use a splatter guard, as it bubbles away like a tub of volcanic gloop, and you may end up with tomato-sauce splodges everywhere. After about 20 minutes, break up any whole tomatoes with the back of a spoon and continue to cook.

After about 45 minutes, add salt and black pepper, to taste. Check the seasoning and add a tiny bit more sugar if you think it needs it. Allow it to cook for a little longer—I reckon it takes a total of 1 hour to reduce properly and become sweet, thick, and unctuous.

SECRETS

You could also add a glass of red wine to the onions once they are cooked, reducing it by half before adding the tomatoes. I sometimes add whole, dried chilies to the softening onion mixture. Once, I had run out of sugar, so I added a splodge of ketchup. Another time, I used Sriracha chili sauce instead, which worked brilliantly.

Other than eating this plain with noodles, I've blended it to make tomato soup; shoved it through a sieve for a more refined sauce; added cream for a pretty, pink pasta sauce; used it as the base for lasagne (see page 70); made a Moroccan-inspired sauce by changing the spicing; used it as a base for curries; made enchiladas with it; baked it in nachos; poured it over baked potatoes ... it's the sauce that just keeps on giving.

PRESENTS FOR GODCHILDREN

When I was little, packages arriving in the post, addressed to me, and covered in stamps, always promised something wonderful. I decided that when I had godchildren of my own, I would be a prolific sender of brown-paper-wrapped packages. Traveling around the world as I do, I pick up gifts from all manner of places, and wing them, tied up with string and good wishes, back to my five godchildren in England. In particular I pick up clothes from other cultures to fire their imaginations. Here are some of my all-star gifts.

SINGAPORE In the heart of Little India is Mustafa Center. It truly is a department store, in that amongst its chaotic aisles and almost impenetrable layout, one can buy mangoes and electronics, lipsticks and gold jewellery. (There's a brilliant kitchen equipment department, too.) And somewhere deep in the heart of the piles of children's clothes are racks of lovely, embroidered salwar kameez, most for less than $25.

145 Syed Alwi Road, Singapore 207704; www.mustafa.com.sg

For satin cheongsams, fans, and those pretty folding paper parasols that I coveted as a child, I head to Chinatown to the tourist-bait stalls of Pagoda Street.

Chinatown MRT

MOROCCO While some derive great pleasure from navigating the narrow lanes of the souks in Marrakesh to haggle endlessly, I've discovered that I prefer the quieter pleasure of shopping in the Ensemble Artisanal where there is a fixed-price store selling only Moroccan embroidered leather slippers in the brightest jewel tones.

Rue de la Kasbah, Marrakesh, Morocco

BARCELONA I lived in espadrilles during the summer as a child, and so I always pick up some godchild-friendly, handmade pairs with pretty, tape-ribbon ties from La Manual Alpargatera in the Barri Gòtic. Founded after the Civil War, it is Barcelona's most iconic espadrille store.

Carrer Avinyó 7, 08002 Barcelona; www.lamanualalpargatera.es

BALI The Carga Lifestyle Store in Seminyak looks like a beautiful Balinese home, hung with red lanterns. Inside are all sorts of treasure from rose-quartz earrings, to wooden platters made from local wood. It's here I bought a lovely handmade doll for Clementine, made by and for a street-kids project. It also stocks silk, batik romper suits by local childrenswear label Coco & Ginger, hand-embroidered party dresses, and frilled underpants for infants.

Jalan Petitenget, 886, Kerobokan; www.cargabali.com

NEW YORK If you have children who are obsessed with the NYPD and the NYFD, then the NYC Firestore is the place to come: they sell anything and everything related to New York's Finest and New York's Bravest. I've found that die-cast fire engines and logo T-shirts go down particularly well, and I am particularly fond of the NYFD toddler T-shirts that say "Stay Back 200 Feet" on the reverse. My feelings exactly, when presented with a chocolate-covered urchin.

17 Greenwich Avenue, New York, NY 10014; www.nyfirestore.com

NEW POTATO, GOAT CHEESE, AND THYME TART

This is the simplest of simple recipes, yet the deliciousness of its transformation—from inedible, raw ingredients to soft, melting, crispy, unctuous, salty moreishness—is something close to alchemy.

I'm afraid it does require a mandoline or a food processor with a slicing attachment unless you possess infinite patience, a very sharp knife, and a true eye for slicing potatoes super thin.

SERVES 4 TO 6

1 small bag new potatoes (approx. 1 lb [500 g])
Approx. 9 oz [250 g] ready-made puff pastry sheet
Butter, for greasing
Flour, for dusting
1 goat cheese (the kind in a log with a rind, not the spreadable stuff), thinly sliced
Several sprigs of thyme
Splash of olive oil
Salt and freshly ground black pepper
1 egg

METHOD

Preheat the oven to 350°F [180°C].

Slice the potatoes. I recommend using either the slicing attachment on a food processor or, like me, risking your fingertips and using a mandoline. It's the work of a few minutes to slice a small bag of new potatoes into uniform pieces. The key word here is uniform: you need the slices to be the same thickness so that they cook through evenly. About the same thickness as a quarter.

Grease a baking sheet with butter. If you plan to serve this tart on a platter rather than the baking sheet, place a piece of baking parchment on the sheet so that you can easily transfer it.

Lay the puff pastry sheet out on a floured board and roll, if needed, until thin but still small enough to fit on the baking sheet. Transfer the pastry over to the greased baking sheet, then lightly score a box about 1 in [2.5 cm] inside the edges. Layer the potato slices onto the pastry within the scored box, and arrange the goat cheese slices on top.

Strew over the sprigs of thyme, splash on some olive oil, and liberally add salt and black pepper.

Beat the egg with a fork and brush over the pastry border.

Bake for about 15 to 20 minutes.

SECRET

New potatoes are the very small, young potatoes harvested at the beginning of the season. Baby potatoes can be substituted if necessary.

WEEKEND ENTERTAINING

A lovely, long lunch with a big group of people is one of my favorite ways to entertain family and friends at weekends. It's comforting, familiar, and relaxed, often going on all afternoon, as we lean back, kick off our shoes under the table (avoiding the children and dogs inevitably hiding there), and get stuck into delicious food.

The traditional English Sunday lunch, in particular, can be daunting to plan and prepare, but with a few tricks and some planning ahead, it's often one of the simplest meals to assemble.

I've been asked to weekend lunches where there has been an appetizer, five vegetables to go with the entrée, umpteen sauces and accompaniments, followed by a dessert and a selection of cheese and bread that I could live off for a week. I say, life is waaay too short. I'd rather be talking to my friends than hovering, puce and sweating, over the stove. Ditch the appetizer, make loads of potatoes, choose two vegetables at the most, and forget any fancy sauces.

In the winter, make a one-dish dessert, like my Eve's Pudding (see page 140), that can be prepared in advance and put in the oven when the entrée is served. In the summer, fruit salad, good ice cream, or a bowl of berries are all perfectly acceptable desserts. Or, make like the French and buy a fruit tart from a pâtisserie.

If you like to serve cheese instead of (or as well as) dessert, choose just one type of something delicious. Buy an oozy slab of Brie at least two days in advance, or a chunk of farmhouse cheddar and serve with grapes, chutney, or membrillo—the Spanish quince paste—and the bread you bought to go with the entrée.

If only one or two people amongst you are vegetarian, please don't worry about providing an extra dish for them: in all my years as a veggie, I was more than happy to eat a plate of delicious Sunday veg. If you *would* like to make something for the vegetarian contingent, make a cauliflower cheese with lots of sauce, or a gratin with

eggs and cream as one of your vegetable sides, then everyone is happy.

On the subject of the night before, try to lay the table then, if you can. I often peel the potatoes then, too (in front of the television) and leave them soaking in cold water overnight. Don't prep any other vegetables in advance: soaking leaches out vitamins, and they can go flabby.

I always have a friend who insists on bringing something with them, and won't take no for an answer, so I suggest they either buy the cheese, something for dessert, or some excellent bread.

Above all, try to relax: it's the weekend, after all ...

LAMB CUTLETS ON
MASHED BUTTER BEANS

In this dish I particularly like the contrast between the melting, tender meat, and the silky-but-rough mashed beans. (It's important to season the meat and the beans properly to really bring out the contrasts.)

Hot or cold, cutlets are always delicious. When I cooked the cutlets for the photo opposite, I had some left over. The next morning I discovered four gnawed bones neatly lined up in the dish: my best friend had decided that they were the perfect post-party midnight snack.

SERVES 4

A little olive oil, for cooking
8 lamb cutlets
Salt and freshly ground black
  pepper
A few snipped chives,
  to garnish

For the butter beans
2 cups [480 g] canned butter
  beans, rinsed and drained
2 Tbsp grassy olive oil

METHOD

Put a heavy pan over high heat—I use a cast iron griddle.

Massage a little olive oil into the cutlets, then put them into the hot pan, in batches. Sprinkle over some salt and a generous grind of black pepper. Cook for 3 to 4 minutes on each side (season each side) for lovely pink middles, and around 5 for well-done meat. Try not to move them around or they won't crisp up properly.

Meanwhile, put all the beans into a large bowl with the olive oil and some salt and pepper, and squash roughly with a fork until they are about half-mashed.

Grab a large platter and turn out the mashed beans onto it. Place the cooked lamb cutlets on top of the beans, pour over any cooking juices, and sprinkle with the chives.

SECRET
A recipe that looks impressive, tastes delicious, and only takes 20 minutes to make is one that everyone should have up their sleeve. And this is one such gem.

ROAST LAMB WITH ANCHOVIES, ROSEMARY, AND GARLIC

I have always cooked roast lamb studded with slivers of garlic and massaged with a paste of mashed anchovies and butter. I promise there will be no fishy reek when you taste this—just deliciousness. (I believe the method originates from Gascony, France.) All you need to make a success of this, is a very sharp paring knife to make slits in the skin into which you insert the garlic slivers. (Use a knife that is too big and your garlic will get lost in the cuts.)

A mortar and pestle is helpful for bashing together the butter and anchovies, but it's certainly not essential.

SERVES 6 TO 8 COMFORTABLY

6 garlic cloves, peeled
Several sprigs of rosemary
1 leg of lamb, approx. 4½ lb [2 kg]
7 Tbsp [100 g] butter, softened
2-oz [50-g] can anchovies in olive oil, drained

METHOD

Preheat the oven to 350°F [180°C].

The cooking time for roast lamb is around 20 to 25 minutes per pound [500 g], plus another 20 minutes on top. So allow about 65 to 75 minutes if you like your lamb nicely pink. If you are more of a well-done person, then add on another 20 minutes.

Slice the garlic into slivers. Pull off little sprigs of rosemary from their stems.

Make a series of incisions in the lamb about 1 in [2.5 cm] long all over the surface, about 2 in [5 cm] apart, and stick the garlic into these, along with sprigs of rosemary.

Mash together the butter and anchovies into a paste, and spread this all over the surface of the meat.

Place in the oven and cook according to the instructions above. Don't forget to factor in another 20 minutes to allow the meat to relax and release its juices, once it has come out of the oven. This will also make it easier to carve.

SECRET

The anchovies are the magic ingredient here. Somehow they become far, far more than the sum of their parts, melting away to a umami-rich note and lifting the flavor of the lamb.

FLEA MARKETS FOR PICKING UP VINTAGE CHINA, GLASS, JEWELRY, AND CLOTHES

USA

MELROSE TRADING POST, LOS ANGELES

The Sunday flea market each week at Melrose and North Fairfax in West Hollywood is as notable for the celebs you can spot trying on vintage cowboy boots and the like, as it is for the actual stalls. It's probably the most expensive flea market I've ever visited, but if you rummage, there are some bargains to be had, especially in homewares.

7850 Melrose Avenue, Los Angeles, CA 90046; open Sunday 9 A.M. to 5 P.M.; www.melrosetradingpost.org

PASADENA ROSE BOWL FLEA MARKET, LOS ANGELES

My absolute favorite place for vintage and second-hand bargains in LA is the Pasadena Rose Bowl Flea Market, which has more than 2,500 stalls. Whether you are searching for vintage Harley Davidson parts or a pretty fifties dress, this is a second-hand goldmine.

Rose Bowl Stadium, 1001 Rose Bowl Drive, Pasadena, CA 91103; open on the second Sunday of each month, 9 A.M. to 4:30 P.M. www.rgcshows.com/rosebowl.aspx

THE ANTIQUES GARAGE, HELL'S KITCHEN FLEA MARKET, NEW YORK

When I lived in New York, I would pop in to The Antiques Garage every weekend to browse the 100-plus vendors. The breadth of items on offer suits my magpie mind perfectly: there are fine silver items, eclectic antiques, furniture, rugs, and prints; plus vintage jewelry, handbags, fabrics, and clothes.

12 West 25th Street (between 6th and 7th Avenues); open Saturday and Sunday, 9 A.M. to 5 P.M.; www.hellskitchenfleamarket.com

BROOKLYN FLEA, NEW YORK

I went to the very first Brooklyn Flea in Fort Greene, and bought vintage jewelry and kitchen bowls. It's now expanded to DUMBO (Down Under Manhattan Bridge Overpass), where you'll find the best stuff for your home. Great food trucks too.

Empire-Fulton Ferry State Park, DUMBO; open Sunday 11 A.M. to 6 P.M.; www.brooklynflea.com

BANGKOK

CHATUCHAK WEEKEND MARKET

One of the largest markets in the world, this has an entire interior design section, as well as an antiques one. Buy a map on arrival and wear flat shoes. I've bought kitchen equipment and wonderful things for my house here.

Next to Kamphaenpecth station (MRT); open Saturday and Sunday, 6 A.M. to 6 P.M.; www.chatuchak.org

UK

LEWES FLEA MARKET, LEWES

Open every day, this is a wonderful place to pick up curiosities and second-hand furniture for the home, as well as, occasionally, vintage fashion and jewelry. I've bought old scent bottles (to use as flower vases) and wonderful vintage china here for bargain prices.

14a Market Street, Lewes, East Sussex BN7 2NB; open daily 10 A.M. to 5 P.M.; www.flea-markets.co.uk

INDOOR FLEA MARKET AT ASHTON GATE STADIUM, BRISTOL

A once-a-month flea market, which attracts both private sellers and dealers from all over the southwest of England, it is particularly good for vintage garden furniture and china, but there is lots of great vintage clothing and jewelry, too.

Ashton Gate Stadium, Ashton, Bristol BS3 2EJ; open one Saturday a month, 9 A.M. to 3:30 P.M.; www.bristolfleamarket.co.uk

FOOLPROOF ROAST CHICKEN

A good roast chicken recipe is an excellent thing to have in reserve. Wherever you may find yourself cooking, it's unlikely that you won't have an oven and a dish that can go inside it. And that's all you need to roast a chicken.

Like so much of my kitchen lore, I learned my roast chicken method from my mother, and it has never failed me. In fact, it's less of a recipe, and more of a kitchen mantra.

It is simply this: allow 20 minutes in the oven per pound [500 g], add an extra 20 on top, and remember that the cooking time should finish about 20 minutes before you wish to eat it, to let the meat (which tightens during cooking) relax, allowing the juices to flow for your gravy.

Once you have that committed to memory, you will always be able to roast a chicken. Of course there are other things that help: I like to massage 7 Tbsp [100 g] butter all over the skin of the chicken, thighs and legs, as well as the breasts; stuff both halves of a lemon inside, and strew some rosemary or tarragon branches around the dish. A liberal application of crunchy salt all over the buttered bird is essential, and a few grinds of black pepper would not go astray.

And that is it: no great secret, no complicated process. But it will give you an incredibly moist chicken; delectable, crisp skin, and lots of buttery, lemony pan juices for the gravy. And the gratitude of your hungry friends and family.

MUSHROOM GRAVY

This intensely savory gravy is perfect for any vegetarian or vegan who may be sitting around your Sunday lunch table: I've found that most vegetarians would infinitely prefer a plate of delicious Sunday vegetables for lunch as opposed to an entirely different entrée. The gravy is the key part of this theory: a dish of vegetables and roast potatoes inevitably needs some sauce and, of course, most gravies contain meat stock and the scrapings from the meat pan. So I've come up with this 100-percent no-meat gravy, which is a hell of a lot easier than having to knock up a separate entrée. Oh, and it freezes like a dream.

MAKES ENOUGH FOR AT LEAST 6 PEOPLE
1 lb [500 g] mushrooms (I like mixed white and portobello)
2 Tbsp vegetable oil
Salt and freshly ground black pepper
2 cups [500 ml] vegetable stock
1 Tbsp dark soy sauce
2 Tbsp cornstarch
4 Tbsp hot water

METHOD
Very finely chop the mushrooms (this is best done in a food processor), reserving a handful of whole white mushrooms.

In a large frying pan, heat the oil and add the chopped mushrooms with a good pinch of salt. Turn the heat down and slowly cook the mushrooms. The key here is to sweat the juices from them without too much evaporation.

Heat the stock and soy sauce in a large saucepan, and when the mushrooms are softened, pour them and their cooking juices into the saucepan with the soy sauce and leave to simmer. Roughly chop the remaining mushrooms into small pieces, add to the pan and cook for another 5 minutes.

Sift (this is very important) the cornstarch into a small bowl and add the hot water, stirring briskly. When mixed, pour into the large saucepan and stir until the sauce thickens. Taste and season with salt and black pepper.

ROAST BOSTON BUTT

When thinking about a Sunday joint of meat for a lunch party, it's always tempting to go for beef —maybe a sirloin or rib—or a leg of lamb, but the former can be wallet-tighteningly expensive, and the latter too small for a large group, and both need precise timings to ensure the meat is cooked the way you like, pink or otherwise.

I like to serve roast pork (although do check with your guests first, as it's the meat that comes with the most dietary issues) because it needs lots of cooking—pink pork is an absolute no-no —which means no complicated timings. It also makes delicious, rich gravy, and of course, gives you a pile of fabulous crackling to chew on.

Most people buy a leg of pork to roast, but I prefer the lesser-known, and much cheaper Boston butt, a cut from the front leg of the pig, just below the shoulder. It is called this not because it is from the rump, but because once upon a time, this cut was stored in barrels.

You can cook it one of two ways: either very long and slow at about 250°F [120°C], so it falls almost in shreds (it's no coincidence that Boston butt is used for barbecue in the Deep South), and that's the way most British cookbooks will suggest; or, you can roast it as you would any normal joint.

You might need to order it from your butcher—this is not a cut that you will find in all supermarkets, especially with the skin on. It depends where you live. He will ask you if you want it on the bone, or off and rolled.

I like getting it on the bone, as it is guaranteed to cook all the way through—the bone acts as a conductor for heat, you get lots more crackling, and I like the generous look of a big joint of meat. Boned and rolled is neater, though, and much easier to carve, as you will get perfect slices.

Either way, tell the butcher how many people you are feeding and he will suggest a suitable piece of meat. (A Boston butt should be able to feed six to twelve people.) Do make sure you ask the butcher to score the skin for crackling. I've forgotten in the past and, take it from me, it's not a simple task getting to grips with a utility knife and a piece of pig.

To ensure lovely, crispy crackling, you need to rub a little oil into the skin, and then rub in lots of flaked salt—I always use kosher salt flakes.

When you pick up your joint from the butcher, ask the exact weight. (It's quite tricky to balance a large joint on a set of domestic scales.) You need to allow 25 minutes per pound [500 g], with an extra 25 minutes on top, and at least 30 minutes to rest out of the oven before you serve it. This allows the meat to relax, making it juicier and easier to carve. I would count on at least four hours in total, and probably five.

To cook it, preheat the oven to 400°F [200°C] and cook the joint for 25 minutes on this high heat to get the crackling off to a good start. Then turn the oven down to 350°F [180°C] for the rest of the cooking time.

I like to carve the meat away from the table. If it is on the bone, I remove the crackling first— you'll find that it lifts off quite easily when a knife slides underneath. Then simply cut the meat into chunks, and use kitchen scissors to cut up the crackling. I pile everything onto a platter, so that everyone can help themselves at the table, family-style.

Roast pork is traditionally served with Applesauce (see opposite). Roast or Hedgehog Potatoes (see pages 100 and 101), cauliflower cheese, and peas or green beans are delicious accompaniments.

APPLESAUCE

This is one of the most versatile sauces and, once you have it under your cooking belt, you can knock it up without a recipe in a matter of minutes for both savory and sweet purposes. I serve it with roast pork and roast goose; it's wonderful spooned over yogurt in the mornings, and I use it in my Blackberry and Apple Trifle (see page 126). It also freezes well, but do remember to label it, as frozen applesauce looks like it could be chicken stock. How many this serves will depend on what you're using it for, but this quantity would be enough for six at Sunday lunch.

SERVES 6

Generous 1 lb [500 g] cooking apples
1 Tbsp + 1 tsp water
1 tsp sugar, or to taste
Squeeze of lemon juice

METHOD

Core and peel the apples and cut into small chunks. Put into a small saucepan with the water, sugar, and the lemon juice and simmer over medium heat. You can either cook it down to a purée, or leave it with some pieces still whole (as you would for the Blackberry and Apple Trifle on page 126).

Do taste the sauce and adjust the sweetness according to your taste: I like mine quite sharp, so you may need to add more sugar if you have a sweet tooth.

CAULIFLOWER PUREE

After years in the culinary wilderness, cauliflower is now recognized as a nutritional wonderfood, lauded for its filling, but low carb-ness and packed with fiber, vitamin C, and potential cancer-busting properties. In this recipe I promptly lower some of that nutritional appeal by loading it with cream and butter. I do like a little indulgence alongside my vitamins.

I cook this at every opportunity: it's wonderful with pretty much every roast meat, makes a perfect, fluffier replacement for mashed potato alongside a stew, and is delicious paired with mushrooms, in any guise. (You'll need a food processor or hand mill. A stick or goblet blender is disastrous as it just chops rather than purées the cauliflower.)

It also makes a lovely soup if you thin it down with vegetable stock and a little whole milk at the end.

SERVES 4 TO 6 AS A SIDE DISH
1 head of cauliflower (approx. 1¾ lb [750 g])
4 Tbsp [50 g] butter, plus a little extra to serve
2 Tbsp heavy cream
Salt and white pepper (not essential, but more aesthetically pleasing than black)

METHOD
Take the cauliflower, cut out the core, and divide into florets. Place in a saucepan and add about 3 in [8 cm] water. Simmer away with the lid on until the cauliflower is completely soft. You do not want any hint of al dente here. Drain the cauliflower over a bowl to catch the cooking water, which you want to keep.

Prepare your food processor or hand mill. Add the cauliflower, butter, and the heavy cream to the mixer bowl. Whizz it all up. If it seems too thick, add a small ladle of the reserved cooking water. Add salt and whizz again. Check the seasoning, adding a little more if necessary.

Serve with 1 to 2 tablespoons butter on top. Snipped chives look pretty, too.

This can be made in advance and reheated, as I often do, to no ill effect, in the microwave.

SHREDDED, SAUTEED BRUSSELS SPROUTS WITH ALMONDS

I loathe and abhor Brussels sprouts. They resemble nothing so much as boiled budgerigar heads and their sulfurous reek is a Proustian return to the school dining room.

Or I thought so until I ate a plate of Brussels, finely sliced and stir-fried in olive oil. What a revelation! Gone was the mushy texture and bitter taste, and in their place, were fresh, al dente greens with just an elusive hint of that brassica bitterness.

You'll need either a mandoline, or a very sharp knife and almost infinite patience.

SERVES 6 AS A SIDE DISH
3 cups [300 g] Brussels sprouts
2 Tbsp olive oil
Heaping ⅓ cup [30 g] slivered almonds
Squeeze of lemon juice
Salt and freshly ground black pepper

METHOD
The secret is to slice the sprouts as finely as possible: I use a mandoline to get them almost paper thin. Then simply add the olive oil to a large frying pan or wok, heat it until it smokes, and tumble in your sliced Brussels sprouts. Don't push them around too much: you want some to stick, so you get a delicious frizzled, browned crispness to the edges. They take 15 to 20 minutes.

Just before you think they are done, toss in the almonds. A squeeze of lemon juice, a little salt, and black pepper and they are ready.

PERFECT ROAST POTATOES

There are many recipes claiming to produce the perfect roast potato, but it really isn't complicated. There is no special ingredient that guarantees results: I don't call for goose fat, polenta, or dustings of flour—just potatoes and hot oil. Olive oil, if you like. Rosemary sprigs in the oil if you fancy it.

The secret to a really crispy outside and melting middle is simple: cook them properly. There is no way you can get perfect roast potatoes in under an hour.

Don't be parsimonious. I allow at least six pieces of potato a head, and usually more. Bank on about 3½ to 4½ lb [1.5 to 2 kg] potatoes for six people. (You'll need the biggest roasting pan you can get in your oven.) Cut them into chunks and parboil them almost to the point of being cooked through. If you forget about the potatoes and overcook them, it doesn't matter; just be careful not to break the pieces up as you drain them.

The single most important part of cooking roast potatoes is to ensure that you slide them into very hot oil. So, preheat the oven to 350°F [180°C], cover the bottom of the roasting pan with ¼ in [0.5 cm] oil, and heat for 5 to 10 minutes until it sizzles.

Then carefully add the potatoes. Do add any broken pieces, as these will be your crispy bits. Be careful, as the oil will spit dreadfully. Turn them over and around so each potato is covered in hot oil. Roast for about 20 minutes, then turn them over. Turn them again at 40. Check them at 1 hour: they may be ready.

When they are perfectly crispy, turn them out into a serving dish and sprinkle some salt over them.

MASHED PEAS

This is not a recipe so much as a serving suggestion, but it is one that lifts the peas from mundane accompaniment to a delicious dish in its own right.

All you need to do is cook the peas, as normal (and I just use garden peas here, not petite sweet peas as I would if serving them straight), put them into a food processor with the leaves from a sprig or two of mint, and pulse two or three times. This chops up the peas but doesn't purée them completely.

Transfer them into a serving dish, add some salt and black pepper, and a little knob of butter. Garnish with some sprigs of mint.

SECRET

No one ever complained about discovering a roast potato in the kitchen a few hours after lunch, so err on the side of generosity and make plenty. Besides, Sunday lunch is all about making people content, and no one was ever made happy by watching their host dole out three potatoes to each guest and then remove an empty serving plate to the kitchen.

HEDGEHOG POTATOES
(OR HASSELBACK, IF YOU MUST)

Okay, purists call these Hasselback potatoes. But I think hedgehog is much more fun. And far more appealing, especially if feeding children or fussy eaters. It's all in the sell, after all. You get a lot of crispiness, which contrasts with the lovely, soft inside: far more crunch, in fact, than a classic roast spud.

There are various ways of making these, and I am sure that the Swedish restaurant that claims them as their invention (Hasselbacken, in Stockholm) would not be altogether happy with my version. But no matter, they pleaseth me and mine, and that is all there is to it. Plus, as a special bonus, my version cooks very quickly, as well as being extraordinarily delicious. Go on, you know you want to …

It is a recipe of simplicity, so I am not going to mess around here. I usually allow at least ½ lb [200 g] per head. I also find that this recipe works equally well with both old and new potatoes.

Potatoes (any kind but not too small; around 3 to 4 per head)
Oil, for roasting (I prefer olive, but vegetable works just as well)
Salt

METHOD
Preheat the oven to 350°F [180°].

Take a very sharp knife and a rounded wooden spoon. Use the sharp knife to halve the potatoes lengthwise (if their shape allows), then place a half, cut-side-down, in the bowl of the spoon. Cut lots of thin, parallel, almost-slices through the rounded side. The cuts should be almost, but not quite, to the bottom. Be careful not to go all the way.

When you are halfway through prepping the potatoes, pour lots of olive oil into a high-sided metal baking pan, and put in the hot oven. (The oil needs to be at least ¼ in [0.5 cm] deep.)

When all your potatoes have been pre-hedgehogged, take out your now-very-hot, oil-filled baking pan and carefully add the potatoes, cut-side-up. I do not recommend adding the potatoes all at once into the oil. Hot oil spits. Tongs are helpful here, if you have them.

Once in the pan, wiggle the potatoes about with a spoon or tongs so they are covered in the lovely, hot oil and then bake for about 45 minutes. Check on them after about 25, and give the pan a good shake to stop the bottoms sticking. Overcooking is better than undercooking.

Once they have been taken out of the oven, sprinkle with lots of crunchy salt.

MUSHROOM SOUP FOR MUSHROOM-OPHOBES

SERVES 4 TO 6

4 Tbsp [50 g] butter

3½ cups [350 g] mushrooms, chopped (I like mixed large, portobello, white mushrooms, and crimini, to get the best flavor)

2 Tbsp chopped flat-leaf parsley leaves (plus extra, to serve, if you like)

1 small garlic clove, chopped

Pinch of nutmeg

4½ cups [1 L] good stock (I'm afraid Jane would turn in her grave, as I use stock powder)

1 thick slice of white bread, torn into pieces (or 4 Tbsp fresh bread crumbs): do not use brown bread as the soup will have bits in it

⅓ cup [75 ml] light cream (plus extra, to serve, if you like)

Salt and freshly ground black pepper

If asked to come up with the menu for my final meal, this soup would be a strong contender for the first course. It's intensely, luxuriously mushroom-y, and is a pleasingly proper, mushroom-gray color with little black flecks from the mushroom gills. When left overnight, it thickens considerably and makes a rather good sauce for chicken.

The recipe below is adapted from one of my all-time favorite cookbooks: Jane Grigson's *The Mushroom Feast*, which I bought in my first year at university, naughtily using the book scholarship I was awarded for my theology degree. (Grigson actually found it first in Elizabeth David's *French Provincial Cooking*.)

What separates it from other mushroom soups is its secret ingredient: a thick slice of bread. The most extraordinary thing is that there is no trace whatsoever of the taste or texture of the bread upon eating.

I've had great success in cooking this soup for avowed mushroom avoiders. And so I'd like to dedicate this recipe to the memory of our friend, Sean Donovan, who was killed in an accident in the summer of our second year at university. He hated mushrooms but loved this soup.

METHOD

Melt the butter in a large saucepan over medium heat, and then add the mushrooms, cooking gently. When the mushroom juices start to run, add the parsley, garlic, and nutmeg and continue to cook. Keep an eye on the heat: you may wish to turn it down so the juices don't evaporate.

Heat the stock in a separate pan.

Add the bread to the stock, and then add the mushrooms. Cook for 10 minutes, then blend in the pan with a stick blender (or use a goblet blender).

Gently heat the cream to a simmer in the now-empty saucepan, then add to the soup.

Adjust seasoning to taste. If I'm serving guests, I like to add a swirl of cream over the back of a spoon and a final dusting of chopped parsley.

LETTUCE SOUP

I know the idea of this might sound a little odd, but do bear with me. I came up with my version because I have neither a bunny rabbit nor a compost heap at home (London apartments not being known for their vast gardens), and I was fed up with throwing away the outside leaves of those lovely Butterhead lettuces.

The soup takes about 15 minutes to make, tops, and tastes rather like a fresh, light pea soup. It's super-healthy, delicious, and astonishingly frugal.

I found that the outside leaves of two lettuces made a sufficient amount for four people for supper and a bit left over. Of course you can use a whole lettuce for this, especially if you are making a quantity of soup. (It's also worth noting that lettuces have much more abundant outer leaves in the summer.) Try Butterhead or romaine. Or a mixture. Whatever floats your lettuce boat.

SECRET
Add a cup of defrosted peas, to thicken, and add a little more flavor. Sorrel would be nice to add to the lettuce, or mint, if you go down the pea route.

SERVES 4 GENEROUSLY
1 onion, finely chopped
Splash of olive oil
Scant 2 Tbsp [25 g] butter
4½ cups [1 L] chicken or vegetable stock (or enough to cover lettuce)
1 whole lettuce (or the outside leaves of 2)
Salt and freshly ground black pepper
Heavy cream, crème fraîche, or sour cream, to serve (optional)

METHOD
Sauté the onion in a little olive oil and the butter, over low heat, for at least 10—probably 15—minutes. You don't want it to color at all, but you do want it properly softened. Don't attempt to speed up the process as you will burn the onion.

Meanwhile, heat the vegetable stock.

Throw the lettuce leaves, washed, and all torn up, in with the onion and pour over the hot stock, to cover the leaves. Bubble away until the leaves are completely softened, then blend with a stick or goblet blender.

Add more hot stock if the soup is too thick. If you accidentally add too much liquid, simmer until it reduces to the required consistency. Season with salt and black pepper.

If you were feeling all fancy, you could add a swirl of cream, crème fraîche, or sour cream.

ASPARAGUS RISOTTO WITH PEA PUREE

I first came across the idea of adding a vegetable purée to a risotto at now shuttered Bar Blanc in Manhattan's West Village just around the corner from my apartment. It adds a lovely depth and color, especially if you use peas, as the green swirls through the dish, adding an extra grassy hit and green color.

SERVES 4 AS AN ENTRÉE OR 6 AS A SIDE DISH

2 fat bunches asparagus
2/3 cup [100 g] petite sweet peas
5 Tbsp [75 g] butter
Approx. 4 1/2 to 6 1/2 cups [1 to 1.6 L] vegetable stock
Salt and freshly ground black pepper
1 small onion or a couple of shallots, finely chopped
2 heaping cups [400 g] risotto rice (I prefer Carnaroli)
Scant 1/4 cup [50 ml] white wine or vermouth

To finish
2 cups [150 g] grated Parmesan cheese
2 Tbsp [30 g] fridge-cold butter

METHOD

Fill a saucepan with about 2 cups of water and bring to a boil. Prep the asparagus by breaking off the ends where they naturally snap. Place the trimmed stalks in a steamer basket above the pan of boiling water, and add the snapped-off ends into the water itself. The trimmed stalks should be cooked al dente—do not let them get soft. (This will only take a few minutes.) Leave the ends simmering away until they're well-cooked.

Cut the tips off the stalks and set aside as a garnish. Cut the remaining asparagus stalks in half. Reserve half, slice the rest into tiny rounds, and set aside.

Turn off the heat under the simmering asparagus ends, fish them out, and discard. DO NOT THROW AWAY THE WATER: you will use it to make the risotto later.

Blend the batch of halved asparagus stalks, peas, almost 1/2 of the butter, 1/2 cup [100 ml] of the stock, plus a spoonful of the asparagus cooking water to a pale green purée using a stick blender or food processor. Taste and season with salt and black pepper. Set aside.

To make the risotto, gently sweat the chopped onion or shallots in the remaining butter over medium-low heat. When the onion has softened (10 minutes or so), add the rice (it should sizzle as it hits the pan) and the white wine or vermouth.

Cook the alcohol until it has all been absorbed by the rice, stirring to make sure it does not stick, and then add a ladle of the stock (including the asparagus cooking water too) at a time. Add more stock as the previous ladle gets absorbed by the rice. Stir, stir all the time so the rice doesn't stick. It takes a while, about 20 minutes, but it's so worth the effort. I recommend the radio in the background, with a glass of the wine used for the risotto in one hand and a wooden spoon in the other. Add the little asparagus rounds about 5 minutes before the risotto is ready.

To finish, beat in the Parmesan and butter with a wooden spoon. This is the *mantecare* stage, a vital element of risotto making which ensures a glossy, smooth finish. Check the seasoning. It'll probably need lots more salt and black pepper. Just before serving, warm the asparagus purée in a small pan, then stir it in so it streaks the risotto. Garnish each plate with the reserved asparagus tips.

SUNCHOKES WITH PEAS, LEMON, AND GARLIC BUTTER

Sunchokes are the tubers of a member of the sunflower family, hence "sunchokes," although they are known as "Jerusalem artichokes" in the UK. I adore them but I may as well be up front about their, er, little surprise. They aren't known as "fartichokes" for nothing. Do not serve these to anyone on a first date unless you really want to make an impression.

Although the little knobbly tubers can look intimidating, they are prepared in the same way as a potato. Peel and chop: done.

While they make the most delicious velvety soups and purées, they are also excellent when, as here, steamed and then fried: the outside goes crunchy, giving way to a soft, yielding middle, which contrasts wonderfully with the pop of the peas. I use petite sweet peas as they are sweeter and have a thinner skin.

SERVES 6 AS AN ENTRÉE OR 8 AS A SIDE DISH

- 1 lb [500 g] sunchokes, peeled and cut into ½-in [1-cm] chunks
- 3 cups [500 g] frozen petite sweet peas
- 1 lemon
- 2 generous Tbsp olive oil
- 2 fat garlic cloves, finely chopped
- 7 Tbsp [100 g] butter

SECRET
Don't be tempted to skip the steaming stage. I've tried doing this: the sunchokes take at least 45 minutes to cook from raw in a frying pan.

METHOD

Steam the sunchokes over a large pan of boiling water for approximately 10 to 15 minutes until they are al dente. (If you don't have a steamer, simply boil them.)

While the sunchokes are cooking, put the frozen peas in a bowl (preferably a metal one) and pour boiling water over them so that they start to defrost. Set aside.

Peel the entire lemon, either using a zester or a small, sharp knife to produce very thin strips of peel. Then cut the lemon in half, and squeeze out the juice into a small bowl, making sure the pits are removed.

When the sunchokes are done, pour the oil into a large frying pan (preferably one with high sides), placed over medium-high heat.

Fry the sunchokes for around 20 minutes until they are crispy on all sides. (Resist the temptation to keep moving them around, as this will stop them crisping.)

Drain the peas and add them to the pan with the lemon zest, garlic, butter, and 1 Tbsp lemon juice. Cook for an additional 5 minutes before serving.

Wonderful
FARMERS' MARKETS & PRODUCE SUPPLIERS

When I am traveling it is always a treat to stay in places where I can cook for myself, whether in a youth hostel (my favorite is the Hi-Marin Headlands, a few miles from the Golden Gate Bridge), a friend's home, or a self-catering home (St Mawes Retreats in Cornwall, UK, are my favorites). That means I have a useful list of markets around the US and UK that I have shopped from on my travels.

SANTA MONICA FARMERS' MARKET, LOS ANGELES

The Central California coast is the fruit and vegetable bowl of America, and some of that produce ends up here: strawberries, piles of unwaxed lemons, fennel waving luxuriant fronds, oranges that smell more orange-y than an English person could think possible.

THE FERRY BUILDING, SAN FRANCISCO

Inside the building are stores, run by independent producers (favorites include Cowgirl Creamery, Acme Bread, and Far West Fungi), but on Tuesday, Thursday, and Saturday the justifiably famous market is open outside. You can buy fruit, vegetables, herbs, flowers, meats, and eggs from small regional farmers and ranchers, many of them certified organic.

UNION SQUARE GREENMARKET, MANHATTAN, NEW YORK

An obvious inclusion, but no less wonderful for all that, and easily accessible for visitors to the city, as well as locals. With 140 regional farmers, fishermen, and bakers, the open air Greenmarket is where many of the city's chefs source the ingredients for their seasonal specials—and it's where I did much of my produce shopping when I lived nearby in the East Village. Look out for New York obsessions like springtime ramps (wild leeks), and don't miss the delicious local artisan cheese stalls. Open Monday, Wednesday, Friday, and Saturday.

DELICIOUS ORCHARDS, COLT'S NECK, NEW JERSEY

Imagine my glee when I discovered I was living a few miles down the road from Jersey's most famous produce store! It's not a farmers' market, but rather a giant hangar selling almost every kind of fresh produce imaginable. Yes, it does ship in fruit and vegetables from all over the US, but it also sells great heaps of local produce, including justly renowned Jersey tomatoes, corn, and apples. Don't miss the photogenic displays of squashes and gourds around Halloween (or the hot apple donuts).

THE TRURO FARMERS' MARKET, CORNWALL

Each Wednesday and Sunday, local producers gather on Lemon Quay to sell some of Cornwall's most delicious offerings. Pedigree pork from Redruth, wild game, Cornish honey, and local vegetables are all available.

THE FIFTEEN SPRING AND AUTUMN FARMERS' MARKET, WATERGATE BAY, CORNWALL

Held twice a year in the main parking lot, you can find fresh fish, local meat, chutneys, artisan cheeses, and bread, as well as cookery demonstrations from local chefs. (I even had a pasta lesson in a tent there once.)

PARLIAMENT HILL FARMERS' MARKET

My local market in North London takes place in a school playground just on the edge of Hampstead Heath, which means I can pick up free-range eggs, a Sunday roast, and delicious bread on the way back from walking the hound.

NEWCASTLE CITY CENTER FARMERS' MARKET

Held outdoors by the towering Grey's Monument on the first Friday of every month, all products on the market must be raised, grown, or produced within a 50-mile radius of the site of the market in order to support local farmers, growers, and producers.

FOOD FOR THE GREAT OUTDOORS

Until I spent time in California, my idea of hell was to be rousted out of bed for a two-hour hike. However beautiful the surroundings, I'd have pleaded an imaginary knee injury, stayed in bed, and worked my way through room service.

I never used to be like this. I did the Duke of Edinburgh's Bronze and Gold Awards at high school, which involved camping, orienteering, and strenuous two- or four-day hikes over the North York Moors.

At 18, I powered up, through and down 7½ miles of interior rainforest to cross Pulau Tioman in Malaysia, in 90 percent humidity. But once I started university, I reverted to my natural state: prone in bed with a novel.

The first inkling I had that I could enjoy exercise in adult life was when I bought a bike in London. Gradually my tentative five-minute outings became half-day expeditions down the London canal paths. Then I moved to Manhattan, bought another bicycle, and became one of those boring cycling evangelists. (Yes, it's so much quicker; yes, you can bike in four-inch stilettos.)

Bicycling has taught me not to be scared of exercise; that I am naturally capable of not collapsing after five minutes of exertion; that it was just exercising in a group, where I thought people were judging my inadequacies and lack of coordination, that I loathed. And that aerobics classes were the work of the devil.

So that brings me to California and to hiking. My dear friend, Judy, forced me up the Santa Lucia mountains and I loved every minute, and became one of those slightly tedious, outdoor evangelists.

And, of course, given that I think about food all the time, I started to think about the kind of food I wanted to eat both when I was on the hoof, and when I was picnicking: because half the fun of a hike is the food stop.

I am always quite surprised when I read suggestions for outdoor food that involve great efforts of assembly; or multiple containers; or messy, sticky foods. The first just seems like hard work, the second too heavy, and the last a magnet for wasps and other creepy-crawlies.

What I want on a picnic or a hike are simple foods that taste delicious in the open air, don't dribble down your arm, and don't require the culinary skills of a chef to assemble. I'm also not very keen on spending hours in the kitchen making tiny pies or similar—food that I can make, pack up, and go out with quickly means heading outside can have an element of spontaneity.

FIVE GREAT PLACES TO GO HIKING IN

LOS ANGELES

1 TOPANGA STATE PARK (for the uphill workout—and the views)
2 WILL ROGERS STATE PARK (for the views of the Pacific Ocean)
3 RUNYON CANYON (because it's hard to believe you are in Hollywood)
4 CHARLIE TURNER TRAIL, GRIFFITH PARK (for the Downtown Los Angeles skyline view)
5 VASQUEZ ROCKS (because they have shot Star Trek TV episodes here)

THREE SANDWICHES
TO EAT ON THE HOOF
WHICH DON'T DRIP DOWN YOUR ARM

I never cease to be astonished at the sandwiches that I see suggested for outdoor activities. The last thing anyone wants is a messy lunch that dribbles everywhere and which, if left untouched, starts to smell.

So, for that reason, I am a big fan of mashing my sandwich fillings, so that nothing can fall out. Another great trick is to use rolls from which you have hollowed out some of the bread, so that the filling can sit securely inside the crust. Pita is also good for this, as you can spread a filling inside without it oozing out of the sides.

FETA, HERB, AND ROASTED TOMATO IN ROLLS

Once I've scooped out some of the inside of a wholegrain roll, I like to fill it with a combination of mashed feta, and roasted or sun-dried tomatoes that have been finely chopped, along with some green herbs—chives are great.

CHEESE AND CHUTNEY ON MULTIGRAIN

One of my favorite sandwiches, but slices of cheese can easily slide out of your sandwich due to the emollient quality of the chutney. So, I suggest grating the cheese (about ½ cup [50 g] per sandwich) and binding it with 1 teaspoon mayonnaise. Spread one side of the inside of the bread with chutney—avoid the lumps, or use a smooth chutney—and the other with your grated cheese and mayo. Press firmly down to seal the sandwich together.

CREAM CHEESE AND HAM IN PETITS PAINS

Mash together 1 Tbsp cream cheese and a slice of ham that you have rolled up and then cut into tiny pieces. Hollow out the petits pains and stuff the mixture inside, being careful not to overfill.

AND ONE EXTRA IDEA, FOR AVOCADO FANS

This is not the sandwich to make for a long hike, but it's great to eat an hour or so after having been made. Simply scoop out the flesh from an avocado and mash it with some salt and a squeeze of lemon juice to stop it discoloring. Then, finely chop together a few sprigs of watercress and a scallion, and mix with the avocado. This mixture is great in granary rolls and, again, I suggest removing some of the crumb to allow the filling to stay securely inside the roll.

CLIMPING, WEST SUSSEX

In the winter this feels like one of the windiest beaches I've visited, but in summer the shingle means that it isn't quite as busy as other beaches nearby, and so long as you take a comfy blanket, it's perfect for a picnic (no sand in your sandwiches).

MAWGAN PORTH, CORNWALL

Not as popular as some Cornish beaches, this quiet and sandy bay, some five miles north of Newquay, is particularly good for a brisk dog-walk very early in the morning. It's equally popular with my sandcastle-building godchildren as it is with the older surfers. I also recommend a brisk, ten-minute haul up to the cliff top to watch the sunset.

CAMBER SANDS, EAST SUSSEX

Possibly Britain's best sandy beach, this was our favorite family expedition as children. Wonderful for sunbathing, this beach offers plenty to do—and there's easy access to ice creams for dessert, too.

MY FAVORITE BRITISH BEACHES FOR A PICNIC

CLEY NEXT THE SEA, NORFOLK

My best friend Emma's mother says that Cley reminds her of Texas, where she grew up: on a perfect summer day it has the same feeling of big blue skies and limitless horizons. Another shingly beach, it can be a bracingly breezy place to sit even in the summer, but if you take a windbreak and anchor it well, it is a glorious spot for a picnic.

BAMBURGH CASTLE BEACH, NORTHUMBERLAND

I went to Newcastle University, and when academic pressures got to us, we would drive up the coast to Bamburgh to picnic on the sands. Known for its beautiful views towards the Farne Islands, its abundant birdlife (look out for the oystercatchers) and its clean water, this is one of the North East's best beaches.

GREENAWAY BEACH, CORNWALL

A blissful, dogs-welcome, coarse-sand beach, tucked up to the north of the family-friendly Daymer Bay. You can't swim here: it's all rock pools, which my sausage dog finds irresistible.

It's often completely deserted, partly because it's a ten-minute walk from nearest parking and there is a steep, often waterlogged, and slippery set rock-hewn steps down to the beach

GRANOLA BARS

I'm afraid that it is a complete fallacy that these are a healthy alternative to sweets. Granola bars may be full of things that are good (or better) for you, like low-glycemic-index carbs, seeds, and nuts, but they are always bound together with something sticky; and whether it's agave or honey, it's still a sugar. That being said, if given a choice between a nutrition-free chocolate bar or one of these delicious snacks, I'd go for the squirrel-friendly one every time.

I've experimented a lot with these—you don't want a super-crumbly bar when you're hiking, so make sure you press them very firmly into the pan before baking. If in doubt, they always benefit from a longer cooking time in the oven than a shorter one.

MAKES 12

2 cups [200 g] rolled oats
7 Tbsp [100 g] butter, plus extra
    for greasing
2 Tbsp cooking oil
3 Tbsp honey or agave nectar
1 Tbsp golden syrup
¼ cup [50 g] light brown sugar
¾ cup [100 g] sunflower seeds
¼ cup [35 g] sesame seeds
¼ cup [35 g] pumpkin seeds
3 Tbsp flaxseeds (optional)
½ Tbsp flaxseed meal
    (optional)
½ cup [50 g] almonds, chopped
8-in square baking pan

VARIATIONS

You could add ⅓ cup [50 g] chocolate chips to the mixture if you have a sweeter tooth. Coconut flakes and little bits of dried apple are good, too.

METHOD

Preheat the oven to 350°F [180°C].

Scatter the oats over a baking sheet and toast in the oven for 25 minutes.

Place the butter and oil in a large saucepan and heat until the butter has melted. Add the rest of the liquid ingredients with the sugar and combine. Remove from the heat the moment the sugar has dissolved.

Grease the baking pan, and line it either with parchment paper or a silicone baking sheet. Make sure that it sticks up over the side of the pan so that you can lift out the granola mix when it is baked.

Add all the dry ingredients to a large bowl, mix together, then pour over the hot oil and syrup and stir thoroughly to combine. Spoon the mixture into the baking pan, and press it very firmly down.

Bake for 25 minutes. Keep an eye on it: when the edges look brown it is done.

Leave it in the pan for 5 minutes to cool, and then turn out onto a cutting board. Immediately cut it into 12 pieces with a very sharp knife; if you leave this process until it is cold, you won't be able to cut it without it crumbling.

Keep in an airtight tin.

SHAKE-IT-UP SALADS IN JARS

These are a big thing amongst my friends in California, who will take any opportunity to eat outdoors, but don't want to lug a formal picnic around with them.

One of the biggest pains about picnicking is the need to pack things in lots of separate jars and bottles so that food doesn't get soggy, waterlogged, or floppy en route. Jar salads solve this problem because the dressing or sauce sits in the bottom of the jar, with the rest of the salad layered over the top, so that until you shake it up—or pour it out—nothing gets mixed together. There's also much less chance of your dressing leaking as there is only a small amount in each jar. Even if the lid becomes unscrewed, the other ingredients should soak it up before there is a chance of spillage. The only requirement is to keep the jar upright. To be honest, these are more of a car thing than a hiking thing: carrying a glass jar around is risky and heavy, but I think of them as the perfect parking lot lunch before a hike.

Mason jars are the ideal containers. But, really, any large jar with a secure lid will do, unless you are mad keen on Instagramming your lunch. (Make sure you sterilize the jars before filling them by putting them in a hot dishwasher or filling them with boiling water.)

The basic rule is dressing first (don't forget to season it), then the heaviest ingredients. Choose the ones that are least likely to soak up the sauce first, with leaves and herbs at the top.

MEXICAN
Avocado and lemon dressing
Chicken
Black beans
Corn kernels
Tomato
Lettuce

CHICKEN
Lemon vinaigrette
Chicken
Cannellini beans
Tomato
Watercress and arugula salad

GREEK
Olive oil dressing with oregano
Feta cheese
Olives
Cucumber
Tomato
Romaine lettuce

CHICKEN NOODLE
Soy and rice vinegar dressing
Chicken
Rice noodles
Bean sprouts
Lettuce

GOAT CHEESE AND CHICKPEA
Olive oil and balsamic dressing
Goat cheese
Chickpeas
Bulgur wheat
Tomato
Arugula

TRAIL MIX FOR JOANNA

When I was 17, Joanna and I got lost on the North York Moors for five hours on our Duke of Edinburgh's Gold Expedition Challenge. It was Easter: raining, cold, and muddy, but we got through our navigational challenges (in the days of flapping wet maps and misted-over compasses) by singing the entire Smiths back catalog, and alternately eating Cadbury's Chocolate Creme Eggs and trail mix.

For those who don't hike, trail mix is a mix of nuts, dried fruit, and sometimes, grains and sweets, which is intended to boost energy. There's no consensus on how it came into existence, although my 17-year-old self was charmed by the discovery that Ray and Japhy in Jack Kerouac's novel, *The Dharma Bums*, ate trail mix.

There's no hard-and-fast rule for the making of trail mix: I just lob in all the things I think I might like to chew on as I tramp up hill and down dale. I do try to avoid adding chocolate and candy: slow-release carbs like nuts are infinitely more useful to the hiker. I'm also going to admit that I make up trail mix to keep me going during fashion week season when, with maybe 12 shows a day to see, there is no time to sit down to eat, and on-the-hoof munching is what keeps me moving forward.

MY PERFECT MIX IS:
Pumpkin seeds
Sunflower seeds
Dried apple pieces, broken into chunks
Dried cranberries
Dried apricots, cut into quarters
Almonds
Cashews
Hazelnuts
Macadamia nuts

CARB-DODGING MINI QUICHES

I'm rather pleased with these little puffy egg things. They are basically a quiche mixture without pastry or cream, which means they are perfect for picnics and outdoors, as there are no crumbly bits to spill down your front. They're also pretty good if you are carb-dodging.

MAKES 6
Butter or cooking spray, for greasing
2 large eggs
¼ cup [25 g] finely grated cheese (I use Parmesan or cheddar cheese)
4 scallions
Lots of black pepper and a pinch of salt
Handful chopped green soft herbs
6-hole cupcake pan

METHOD
Preheat the oven to 350°F [180°C]. Either wipe a little butter around each hole in the cupcake pan or, if you're in a particularly diet-minded mood, use cooking spray.

Then, to produce 6 of these, beat the eggs together and grate in the cheese, using the finest grater you have (a little goes further this way).

Chop the scallions, including most of the green, and mix together with the egg and herbs, along with lots of black pepper and a pinch of salt.

Divide the mixture between the cupcake holes. It should half-fill each one. Put into the hot oven and cook for about 10 minutes until they have all puffed up.

They will deflate as they cool, but they still taste just as good.

VARIATIONS
¼ cup [25 g] of any of the following can also be added: chopped ham, cooked mushrooms, cooked leeks, or onions.

GOOD THINGS IN THERMOS FOOD JARS

The discovery of wide-necked Thermos food jars was a revelation to me. I'd tried putting chunky soups in a standard drink bottle, but something always got stuck inside, and you certainly couldn't put anything that wasn't liquid in them.

The possibility of a wide-necked jar suddenly means that picnics can get a lot more exciting, so you no longer need to trail endless boxes and bags to create something delicious on site. As long as you prep your jar properly first by warming it with boiling water, whatever you put in should stay warm all day.

Hot food needn't be restricted to winter picnics or sitting in the car at a point-to-point in the countryside. My favorite things to add are baby potatoes with a good dose of butter, some salt, and mint. They go particularly well with quiches and salads. Petite sweet peas prepped the same way are excellent, too.

That being said, the following recipes from this book are perfect for putting in a jar:

- Zucchini and Pea Orzotto (page 76)
- Winter-Warming Beef, Barley, Mushroom, and Carrot Stew (page 41)
- Pork, Chorizo, and Lima Bean Stew (page 42)
- Mushroom Soup for Mushroom-ophobes (page 102)

Do think hard about including pastas in sauces, and starches that might continue to absorb liquid and thus go soggy. Barley is bombproof, so it will keep its shape; risotto rice will not.

JEWELED JELLIES IN JARS

What a lovely thing to take on smart picnics: I'm thinking outdoor theater or concerts in the summer, where something a little more elegant than a package of sandwiches is called for. (However, best not to attempt these in a heatwave, unless you particularly like drinking your jelly.)

I use agar-agar to set these, rather than gelatin. I don't like the smell of the latter when it is cooking and I don't see the point when a perfectly good alternative is available. It also means you don't have to worry about any vegetarians in the alfresco group.

Adhering to my no-faff mantra, these are very quick to make, and to set—they are firm in about 45 minutes. You do need to make the jelly in layers—don't worry, these won't show when they set—as otherwise, all the fruit floats to the top.

MAKES 4 TO 6 LITTLE JELLIES

2 cups [500 ml] cold water
⅓ cup [70 ml] elderflower syrup (found in specialty grocers and online)
2½ heaping Tbsp agar-agar
2 handfuls berries to set in the jelly; I've used blueberries and raspberries
4 to 6 little preserving or screw-top jars

METHOD

Pour the cold water and elderflower syrup into a saucepan and sprinkle the agar-agar on top. Do not mix. Bring slowly to boiling point and when it reaches a boil, stir to ensure all the agar-agar flakes have dissolved—this may take up to a further 5 minutes.

While the mixture is heating, place a few berries in each of the jars. When the hot jelly mixture is ready, carefully pour it to just cover the first layer of fruit.

Allow this first layer to set, then reheat the remaining jelly to liquidity again, drop in some more berries and, again, cover them with jelly. Repeat as many times as necessary to fill the jar—I try to aim for 3 layers.

These will set in about 45 minutes, but I do recommend keeping them in the fridge overnight to ensure a firm set.

SECRET
Don't be tempted to use sliced strawberries: they leach their color into the jelly.

SWEET THINGS

When I was a little girl, I was fascinated by the Cordon Bleu series of cookbooks, with their navy blue and white covers. There were two in particular: one called *Hot Puddings* and one called *Cold Desserts*. *Hot Puddings* intrigued me because it did, after all, contain sugar, chocolate, and other ingredients appealing to the infant mind.

But as much as I love a hot dessert (or "pudding" as we Brits call it), it was *Cold Desserts* that exercised a mystic thrall over me. I used to gaze lovingly at the meringue concoctions, glasses of trifles, lavish use of whipped cream, and luscious strawberries that appeared on almost every page.

Although I obsessively bookmarked them with scraps of paper, I don't remember either myself or my mother actually cooking from them. Those desserts were from the realms of fantasy, not reality.

As an adult, re-reading those books awakened my love of desserts, but it didn't instill any desire to spend hours in the kitchen wielding a pastry bag, or constructing complicated choux towers.

Instead, my taste runs towards a simpler approach: one where you can cook ahead, or serve up a large bowl or platter, into which everyone can dive.

My presentation may be simple, but there has been no compromise elsewhere: I feel strongly that if you are simplifying the processes, then the ingredients must be excellent in themselves, and that there is no excuse for serving an unattractive plate of food. It's wonderful how a sprinkle of powdered sugar, a grating of chocolate, or a few mint leaves can perk up a dish. That being said, no artful smears, towers, or unnecessary sauces, please.

On those occasions where you want a bit of warmth and comfort, you can't beat a hot dessert. There are so many occasions where it's the perfect end to a meal: a long, leisurely Sunday lunch in winter; supper around the kitchen table with friends; or when you just want to dive headfirst into some comfort food. There is something intensely reassuring about them, maybe because we ate them so often in school dinners, or as children.

Hot desserts are often simple to make: there's no waiting around for mousses to set, or ice cream to harden, and just because a dessert is served warm doesn't mean you need to make it there and then: you can either prepare it in advance and put it in the oven when you serve the entrée, or you can cook the entire thing beforehand and just reheat it.

I'm including some gooey, fruit-packed cakes here because I think they are underutilized at the end of a meal: cake isn't just for tea, and whipping up a cake batter can be a lot quicker than constructing a pudding from scratch.

British traditionalists always want custard sauce with their dessert (or maybe *crème anglaise* if they are feeling fancy). But don't forget the appeal of heavy cream; decadent spoons of whipped cream; or silky-smooth vanilla ice cream—all of these bring a wonderful, cool contrast to the steamy sweetness of a hot "pudding."

MIXED BERRY SUMMER PUDDING

It took me a Very Long Time to get my head around the English classic, summer pudding: I thought the idea of fruit-juice-soaked soggy bread utterly revolting. Then I needed to knock up a dessert for a last-minute lunch, and all I had at home was a loaf of good white bread and several baskets of berries. Clearly, a summer pudding was the solution. Because I couldn't bear to watch other people eat and deprive myself, I tentatively forked up a mouthful.

Reader, I loved it. Somehow, the bread doesn't taste soggy, so much as just saturated with fruit.

Traditionally, a summer pudding contains just raspberries and red currants, but I added both black currants and resolutely non-traditional blueberries, which I think add a little texture, as well as relief from the sharpness of the currants. One should not be tempted to try using strawberries here (they just turn to mush). And really, this is not the time to use up forgotten berries—summer pudding is designed to show off perfect summer fruit, so use the best you can find.

SERVES 6 GENEROUSLY

1¾ lb [750 g] **summer berries**
   (my favorite combination is:
   1 cup [100 g] **red currants,**
   1 cup [100 g] **black currants,**
   3½ cups [450 g] **raspberries,**
   1 cup [100 g] **blueberries)**
½ cup [100 g] **granulated sugar**
7 medium slices of good white
   bread (a sandwich loaf is
   perfect)
Heavy cream, to serve
Standard pudding basin

SECRET
Only use very good white bread for this—definitely not sliced bread which will turn into a disgusting soggy mess after a stint soaking up juicy berries. Yuck!

METHOD

Using the tines of a fork, slide the currants off their stems, and pick over the raspberries and blueberries. Place a medium saucepan over low heat and pour in the fruit and sugar. Cook for 5 minutes, no more, until the berries have started to release their juices.

Meanwhile, cut the crusts off the bread. Using a pastry cutter or by cutting around a small plate, cut 1 bread circle to fit the base of the pudding basin, and use this to line the bottom of the bowl. Then line the sides with pieces of bread, cut to fit, making sure there are no gaps.

Remove a couple of tablespoons of the berry juice from the saucepan and reserve. Pour the fruit and their juices into the bread-lined bowl and create a lid over the top using the rest of the bread.

Place a small plate over the top of the pudding and weigh it down with a can of food. Ideally, leave this overnight, although I have found that you can get a good result if you make this about 3 hours before serving.

When you are ready to serve it, simply slip a knife around the edge of the basin, remove the plate, and replace with an upturned serving plate. Invert the basin, tap the bottom hard and, hopefully, your summer pudding will slide out onto the plate. You will inevitably find some white patches on the bread, especially if you haven't been able to leave it overnight, so spoon the reserved juice over those parts of the pudding.

Serve with thick, or pour lovely, thick heavy cream in a gentle stream over each portion.

PATRIOTIC PAVLOVA

I first made this for a Thanksgiving lunch in Los Angeles where, in direct contradiction of urban legend, people do eat both cream and sugar. Especially when it looks as pretty as this.

I was scared by the idea of making pavlovas for years: I always thought the meringue would break, that it was all far, far too complicated. That is, until I realized that this is not only very simple and quick to make, but can be done the night before, which dramatically decreases stress in the kitchen. You do need a handheld electric whisk or stand mixer both for the egg whites and for the cream—unless, of course, you particularly want to spend half the day with a hand whisk.

If raspberries and blueberries do not appeal, there are plenty of other toppings that work beautifully on a pavlova. Sliced nectarines and raspberries are a lovely combination in the summer, as are plums and slivered almonds in the colder months.

SERVES 6 TO 8

4 egg whites
Pinch of fine salt
1 heaping cup [225 g] granulated sugar
1 tsp white wine vinegar
1 heaping tsp cornstarch
1 tsp vanilla extract
1¼ cups [300 ml] heavy cream
1 basket raspberries
1 basket blueberries
Powdered sugar, for dusting (optional)

METHOD

Preheat the oven to 350°F [180°C], and line a baking sheet either with baking parchment or, better still, a silicone baking sheet. (This will also decrease stress, as the meringue just slips off and minimizes any chance of breakage.)

Put the egg whites and salt into a scrupulously clean, dry mixing bowl, or the bowl of a stand mixer. Beat with a handheld electric whisk or the mixer until the egg whites are super-fluffy (the stiff white should not drop off the whisk), but do be careful not to overbeat as they will start to separate. Then, keeping the whisk running, add the sugar a spoonful at a time.

Then whisk the vinegar, cornstarch, and vanilla into the glossy mixture as quickly as you can.

Using a large spoon, heap the meringue mixture onto the baking sheet in a rough oval, making a slight depression in the middle, which will hold the fruit later.

Turn the oven down to 300°F [150°C], and bake the meringue for 45 minutes.

When the baking time is up, turn off the oven and leave the meringue inside to cool. (I usually make this the evening before, and leave it in there overnight.)

Very carefully remove the meringue from the baking sheet, peeling off the liner as you go, and slide onto your serving dish. Do check that the dish is big enough, as meringue is too delicate to overhang and will break, as I have found out to my cost.

Just before serving, whip the cream, but do not leave it whirring away as you do something else, as the difference between lovely, light, and floppy, and solid cheese-y cream is a second of inattention. Generally the cream will be whipped before it looks done, so keep checking.

Spread the cream over the meringue.

Pick over the fruit, and then toss it randomly over the cream. Some sifted powdered sugar looks pretty, if you like.

THE BROADWAY PANHANDLER, MANHATTAN, NEW YORK

Just below Union Square, and a few blocks from Strand Bookstore (see page 58) and its excellent cookery section, this is, hands down, my favorite cookshop in the world. It's not so big that you become overwhelmed, or so small that they have over-edited their stock: there is just enough of anything you might possibly need in your kitchen.

Whether I am seeking a very particular size in metallic cupcake cases, or a new kitchen apron, this store is always my first port of call. It also has a very serious selection of knives, and offers a sharpening service too.

65 East 8th Street, New York, NY 10003

BLACKBERRY AND APPLE TRIFLE

My grandfather loved trifle, so my mother always made him a proper English trifle from scratch, layering up pieces of homemade whisked vanilla cake, liberally soaked with sherry and spread with jam, fresh fruit, crème anglaise, and a drift of whipped cream, garnished with slivered almonds.

My version is a more modern take, but don't worry: it still sticks to the traditional trinity of custard sauce, cream, and cake. I just prefer to use a crème pâtissière as it is much thicker, creating a separate custard layer, rather than oozing through the entire dish.

Instead of sherry I use the delicious French blackberry liqueur, crème de mûre, which really brings out the blackberry flavor of the dessert, although you could happily substitute more easily available crème de cassis—or revert to sherry if that is what you have. There's no need to be prescriptive with a trifle. (If you are booze-free, you can use apple juice instead.)

I'm afraid that I don't make my trifle cake: I have discovered that storebought pound cake is perfect. It's dense enough not to go soggy, and tastes wonderful when saturated with booze.

In winter I make the trifle with a package of frozen mixed berries—frozen blackberries are almost impossible to find, and these mixed ones are a very successful substitute.

The key to not being stressed by a trifle is to remember that it is really a series of separate ingredients, piled together in a very deep glass dish, most of which can be prepared the day before if necessary.

SERVES 8 TO 10

Crème Pâtissière (see opposite)
2 quantities Applesauce (see page 97)
2 cups [250 g] frozen or fresh blackberries
Squeeze of lemon juice and 2 tsp sugar, if using fresh blackberries
Approx. 1 lb [450 g] storebought pound cake
¼ cup [50 ml] crème de mûre (or crème de cassis, or apple juice)
5 Tbsp good blackberry jam (e.g., Fresh Blackberry Jam, see page 146)
2½ cups [570 ml] heavy or whipping cream
1¼ cups [100 g] slivered almonds

METHOD

First make the Crème Pâtissière so that it has time to cool. Then make the Applesauce, leaving some chunkiness, and allow to cool.

Defrost the fruit if using frozen, setting a few berries aside to decorate. If using fresh fruit, set some aside, then put into a pan with a squeeze of lemon juice and 2 tsp sugar. When the sugar has dissolved, remove from the heat and allow to cool.

Cut the pound cake into mini slabs about the length of your middle finger and use them to line the bottom of a trifle dish, or large, deep, glass serving bowl. Douse the cake with the alcohol or juice. Spread the jam over the cake. Now pile the fruit (it must be cool) over the cake, followed by the Applesauce. This gives a nice, smooth layer over which to pile the Crème Pâtissière, which goes on top next.

Now whip the cream very carefully: it is very easy to overwhip. You are aiming for a nice, floppy texture; generally it is ready before it looks it, so stop and stir it through before you think it's fully whipped. Spoon on top of the Crème Pâtissière.

Decorate the cream with the whole blackberries, and scatter over the slivered almonds.

THREE GLORIOUS SHERRIES

Like so many people, my first sip of sherry came out of a blue glass bottle and accompanied a piece of Christmas cake. It wasn't until I visited Jerez de la Frontera in Spain that I realized that sherry's variety means it can be as delicious with roast beef and cheese as it can with desserts and cake.

Fino
The driest, palest and youngest of all sherries, chilled fino is perfect with tapas, but if you travel to Jerez you will see it drunk everywhere as you would a white wine. (Beware its deceptive 15 percent alcohol content.)

Pedro Ximénez
My absolute favorite: made from the grape of the same name, this is one of the world's oldest dessert wines. This rich, dark, sweet sherry tastes like essence of macerated raisins, and is sublime poured over vanilla ice cream.

Matusalem
Produced in very small quantities, Matusalem is a dark Oloroso sherry, made from a blend of 75 percent Palomino and 25 percent Pedro Ximénez grapes. Aged for over 30 years, it has a rich, sweet finish, which is wonderful with strong cheeses and tastes lovely against cooked apples.

CREME PATISSIERE

2 cups [500 ml] whole milk
1 tsp vanilla extract
4 egg yolks
6 Tbsp powdered sugar
4 Tbsp cornstarch

Heat the milk and vanilla extract in a saucepan. Meanwhile, beat the egg yolks together with the powdered sugar and the cornstarch. When the milk is simmering, slowly dribble the egg mixture onto it, whisking away.

It will eventually thicken into perfect crème pâtissière. Scoop into a dish to cool. And that's it.

CHOCOLATE ORANGE MOUSSE

Chocolate mousse was, hands-down, my family's favorite Sunday-lunch dessert when my sister and I were little. My father loved it because he only likes dark chocolate; my sister and I because it seemed grown-up and therefore very appealing; and my mother because it was simple and quick to make.

This is not a light and fluffy mousse, but rather a dense, indulgent affair. My mother always used an Arabella Boxer recipe, from her amazing 1960s classic *First Slice Your Cookbook*. This fascinated me as a child because it was spiral-bound and cut into three separate, horizontal sections—appetizers, entrées, and desserts, so you could create a perfect three-course menu. I have adapted her recipe here.

The main thing to remember is that you need to make this in advance. It can be made the night before and put in the fridge, but I find that if I beat this up before I put the Sunday roast in the oven, that's plenty of time for it to firm up—about two hours before serving.

SERVES 8

- 4 oz [120 g] bittersweet chocolate (70% cocoa solids), plus extra to decorate
- 4 eggs, separated
- 1 Tbsp Cointreau or freshly squeezed orange juice (optional)
- 2 tsp granulated sugar

METHOD

Break the chocolate into pieces and put in a heatproof bowl over, but not touching, a pan of simmering water. When the chocolate begins to melt, turn the heat off, beat the chocolate with a wooden spoon, and allow to cool.

Scoop the cooled, melted chocolate into a large mixing bowl.

Beat the egg yolks together with a fork, and stir quickly into the melted chocolate mixture, followed by the liqueur or juice.

In a scrupulously clean, dry bowl, whisk the egg whites into firm peaks: I use a stand mixer or handheld electric whisk. (It will take forever to do this with a hand whisk or egg beater.) Then whisk in the sugar.

Whisk one-third of the egg whites into the chocolate mixture, until combined. Using a metal spoon, fold the rest of the egg white very gently into the mixture, until just combined (be careful not to overbeat).

Scoop into a pretty serving bowl and refrigerate for at least 2 hours or overnight, until set. Sprinkle over finely grated chocolate. (I like to use my grandmother's cut-glass bowl.)

INDIVIDUAL CHOCOLATE TRIFLES

These are the perfect make-ahead desserts for which you need the basic Chocolate Orange Mousse recipe opposite (leaving out the Cointreau or juice), half a quantity of the Brownies (see page 150), as much whipped cream as you crave, and some chocolate for grating, or slivered almonds or chopped nuts.

For six people, split the mousse between six stemmed glasses, and allow to set (minimum two hours). Then cut the brownies into small chunks, and divide evenly among the glasses. Top with whipped cream, and grate over some chocolate.

I use glasses for these mini trifles because I like seeing the layers of mousse, brownie, and cream, but there is no reason why you can't make them in whatever vessels you have handy: I've used both teacups and small bowls.

SUMMER BERRY TART

While I've been making classic quiches for years with great success, I've always been slightly scared by the idea of making a proper pâtisserie-type tart. They require two ingredients which are notorious for going wrong: *pâte brisée* (an extremely short, buttery pastry which can be a pig to work with as, if you get it too short, it has to be pressed into place rather than rolled); and *crème pâtissière* (proper confectioner's custard which splits if you so much as look at it the wrong way).

It does not help that my mother makes extraordinarily good pastry, and thinks nothing of knocking up a tart at the last minute. Leave it to the experts I've always said, or do as the French and buy one from your local pâtisserie. So, I'd never made *pâté brisée* or *crème pâtissière* before. And, as I don't much like hot eggy runny custard, I always presumed that I didn't like *crème pâtissière*. How wrong was I? Last year I discovered that I loved it **and** that neither the *crème* nor the pastry are nearly as difficult to make as I had thought. So here you are—and what could be prettier?

SERVES 8 TO 10

1 quantity Crème Pâtissière
(see page 127)
Berries, to decorate (I use
approx. 2¼ cups [300 g]
raspberries, 2 cups [200 g]
blueberries and 1¾ cups
[350 g] sliced strawberries)

For the pastry
2 cups + 1 Tbsp [250 g]
all-purpose flour
7 Tbsp [100 g] fridge-cold
butter, cut into small pieces
1 egg yolk
3 generous Tbsp [50 ml] cold
water with a pinch of fine salt
Heaping ⅓ cup [50 g]
powdered sugar
*10-in [26-cm] fluted tart pan,
preferably nonstick and loose-
bottomed, greased*
*Ceramic baking beans (you can
use lentils or rice if you don't
have baking beans)*

METHOD

First make the Crème Pâtissière so that it has time to cool.

Throw the pastry ingredients into a food processor and pulse until it comes together, keeping an eagle eye on it so it isn't overworked.

If making by hand, place the flour in a large mixing bowl and add the butter. Using the fingertips of one hand, rub the butter into the flour until it resembles bread crumbs. Then make a well in the center and add the egg yolk, salted water, and powdered sugar. Mix together with your hands. The moment the pastry comes together, dump it onto a floured board, push into a ball, wrap in plastic wrap, and put into the fridge to rest for an hour.

When you are ready to assemble the tart, preheat the oven to 350°F [180°C].

Roll the rested pastry out on a floured surface using a rolling pin. It needs to be a circle slightly bigger than the tart pan. Lift the pastry loosely around the rolling pin, and unroll it directly into the pan. Press it into shape, leave about ½ in [1 cm] over the edge, and trim off any remaining overhang with a knife.

Line the pastry with baking parchment, and fill with baking beans to stop the pastry rising during baking. Bake for 25 to 35 minutes, depending on your oven. Allow the pastry to cool slightly before removing the beans on their paper, gently taking the pastry shell out of the pan, and transferring it onto a wire rack to cool. Using a sharp knife, trim the overhanging pastry around the edges.

When the pastry shell is cold, pour in and spread out the crème pâtissière, and spend a fun 10 minutes decorating with the berries.

CHERRY ETON MESS

When I spent the summer in New Jersey a few years ago, this was the dessert I'd make to eat outdoors, under the trees. It makes me think of long, sunny days and friends. The combination of crushed meringues, cream, and soft fruit is one that rarely fails to please.

I love making meringues: I have a passion for that dense marshmallow-y chewiness in the interior you can't get in commercial or restaurant offerings. When I was little, my mother, the ace cook, used to make the chewiest meringues in her AGA oven and sandwich them together with dense whipped cream for birthday parties.

That being said, Eton Mess works perfectly well with storebought meringues. (Buy the nicest ones you can afford.)

Strawberries are the traditional fruit in an Eton Mess, but I have a few other suggestions.

SECRET

If you're the kind of person who likes marshmallow-y meringues, leave them to cool in the oven for only 30 minutes. For the dry-and-crispy-centered-meringue lovers out there, leave your meringues in a cooling oven for as long as possible.

SERVES 6

8 egg whites
Pinch of fine salt
2½ cups [500 g] granulated sugar
2 tsp white wine vinegar
1 heaping Tbsp cornstarch, sifted
1 tsp vanilla extract
2½ cups [560 ml] heavy cream
1 cup [250 g] cherries, pitted and halved, or one of the variations below

VARIATIONS

- Mixed berries: raspberries, red currants, black currants, blueberries
- Passion fruit and mango
- Chopped apricots and slivered almonds
- Persimmon and mint
- Strawberries and mint

METHOD

Preheat the oven to 350°F [180°C] and line 2 baking sheets with baking parchment.

Pour the egg whites and salt into a scrupulously clean, dry mixing bowl, or the bowl of a stand mixer. Beat with a handheld electric whisk or the mixer until the egg whites are super-fluffy (the stiff white should not drop off the whisk), but do be careful not to overbeat as they will start to separate. Then, keeping the whisk running, add the sugar a spoonful at a time.

Then whisk the vinegar, cornstarch, and vanilla extract into the glossy mixture as quickly as you can.

Heap large spoonfuls of the meringue mixture onto the baking sheets, turn the oven temperature down to 300°F [150°C] and bake for 30 minutes.

When the cooking time is up, turn off the oven and leave the meringues inside to cool for 30 to 60 minutes.

You can serve this either piled onto a large platter for everyone to help themselves, or you can divide into individual bowls. I sometimes use vintage tea cups.

Pull the meringues into chunks.

Whip the heavy cream to soft peaks using a handheld electric whisk or a balloon whisk (and a lot of elbow grease). Spoon the cream and meringue chunks into the platter or cups, and spoon the cherries over.

WARM APPLE AND HAZELNUT STREUSEL CAKE

I first made this cake when I discovered a package of hazelnut flour from the New York deli, Dean & Deluca, languishing in the back of my kitchen cupboard. Upon further investigation, it turned out to be a fancy name for ground hazelnuts, and I thought they would be perfect in a cake with apples, as ground nuts add a lovely, gooey quality.

While it eats beautifully cold as a picnic cake, I do think it comes into its own in the winter months as a dessert, served warm from the oven, with a blanket of either cold heavy cream or silky egg custard sauce.

I think slightly tarter dessert apples like McIntosh are best here. It's also a fantastic way to use up those slightly past-it apples in the fruit bowl. If you can't lay your hands on ground hazelnuts, then this cake works just as beautifully with ground almonds.

SERVES 8 TO 10

1 cup [225 g] butter, softened, plus extra
**   for greasing**
1 lb [450 g] apples
Juice of ½ lemon
Heaping ¾ cup [175 g] granulated sugar
¼ cup [50 g] soft brown sugar
1 tsp vanilla extract
3 eggs
1¾ cups + 1 Tbsp [225 g] self-rising flour
2 tsp baking powder
1 tsp ground cinnamon
Heaping ⅓ cup [30 g] ground hazelnuts
Powdered sugar, to serve

For the streusel topping
2 Tbsp ground hazelnuts
2 Tbsp soft brown sugar
1 Tbsp melted butter
1 tsp ground cinnamon
Deep, 8-in [20-cm] springform cake pan

METHOD

Preheat the oven to 350°F [180°C].

I'm a big fan of reusable silicone pan liners, which mean you don't need to grease or line your pan. If you don't have a silicone liner, grease the cake pan, and line the sides and base with baking parchment. (This cake will really stick otherwise.)

Peel, core, and chop the apples into ½-in [1-cm] chunks. To stop them going brown, pour the lemon juice over and mix together.

You can do this next bit by hand but, seriously, unless you are looking for ways to incorporate exercise into every moment of your daily routine, I highly recommend a food processor or electric mixer. Put the butter and both sugars into a stand mixing bowl and beat together. You are aiming for a light and fluffy mixture.

Add the vanilla extract, and then 1 egg at a time, along with a spoonful of flour—this will prevent the mixture curdling.

Mix together the baking powder, cinnamon, and ground hazelnuts with the rest of the flour, and add to the cake mixture one heaping spoonful at a time, being careful to stop beating the moment the flour has been incorporated. (Overbeating will lead to a heavier cake.)

If using a food processor, scoop out the batter into a bowl and add the apple pieces. Fold them all together. If using a stand or hand mixer, just add the apples to the mixing bowl and fold together. Make sure that the apple pieces are distributed throughout the cake mixture.

Don't worry if the mixture is stiffer than you would want in a pound cake. This is both because the apples will leach their juice during baking, and because you want the mixture to hold the pieces, otherwise they will sink to the bottom of the cake.

Spoon the mixture into the lined cake pan.

Lick the cake bowl.

Make sure that the top of the cake mixture is level-ish (use a spatula or the back of a spoon).

Mix together the ingredients for the streusel topping and sprinkle over the top of the cake. Don't worry about it clumping. This is good, as it will make for crunchy bits.

Put in the oven for 45 minutes. I find that the top browns very quickly, so I add a piece of paper over the top of the cake at the 45-minute mark, and then bake for another 15 minutes to make 1 hour total.

As oven temperatures can vary, do test the cake for doneness at 45 minutes with a toothpick. If the cake is baked, the toothpick will come out clean. Test in several places around the center of the cake, because if you hit a piece of apple, the toothpck will come out clean, giving a false positive. If there is any hint of batter on the toothpick, it needs more baking. Check again after 5 minutes.

When the cake is done, remove from the oven, undo the springform clip, remove the side ring, and gently slide the cake from the metal base onto a wire rack.

Serve warm, with powdered sugar dusted over the top.

MY GODMOTHER ROSALIND'S POACHED PEACHES IN WHITE WINE SYRUP

Unless it's the height of summer, peaches invariably disappoint. They go from rock hard to fluff in seconds, missing that perfect moment where one bite sends juice cascading down your chin.

Poaching indifferent peaches is an excellent way to turn them into something quite lovely. Peeling them is a little bit of a production, but it's worth the effort, especially as, if you choose peaches with a dark-pink skin, the color imprints itself onto the flesh beneath. My beloved godmother taught me how to peel and poach a peach one summer vacation when I was about twelve: it's actually very easy to do. Don't bother trying this with imported peaches in the dead of winter—it's almost impossible to shuck the skins off the bullet-like fruit.

If you like, go the whole hog and make peach melba—as my Norfolk granny would do if we begged, with a ball of vanilla ice cream perched over each half, and raspberry purée poured over it all.

SERVES 4

Generous 1½ cups [375 ml] water
1 vanilla bean (optional)
2 cups [500 ml] white wine
¼ cup [50 g] granulated sugar
4 peaches
Heavy cream, to serve

METHOD

Place the water, vanilla bean, if using, wine, and sugar in a heavy-bottomed saucepan and bring to a boil. Place the peaches in the liquid, reduce the heat to a gentle simmer, and poach for 20 minutes, making sure that you move the peaches around occasionally so that they cook evenly.

Remove them from the pan with a slotted spoon and allow to cool. Peel the skin off very carefully.

Put the pan back on the heat and boil the liquid until it has reduced by about half and you have a thick syrup. Allow to cool slightly.

I serve these in a little glass bowl, with a spoonful of syrup poured over, and heavy cream in a pitcher nearby.

HOT CROSS BUN
BREAD-AND-BUTTER PUDDING

One summer in France, I found a big bag of hard, stale pains au chocolat hiding in a kitchen cupboard in our vacation home. I cannot abide waste, so I cut them into fat slices, put them in a dish with some large chunks of dark chocolate that I happened to have lurking in my purse for emergencies, and poured over a rough-and-ready custard sauce: a mixture of eggs, sugar, cream, and milk. Basically the traditional British bread-and-butter pudding, but with French pastries. It was one of the most delicious things I've ever eaten.

Hot Cross Buns are small sugar-glazed, currant and spice yeast-risen buns, traditionally eaten over Easter in the UK. They can occasionally be found in specialty bakeshops in the US, or can be made easily at home.

In the absence of these delicious buns, I would suggest subbing in around twelve inch-wide slices of cinnamon bread, lightly buttered, sandwiched together, and cut in half. Place the 6 sandwiches in the dish, slightly overlapping each other.

The glorious thing about this recipe is that when you remove the dish from the oven, the Hot Cross Buns or bread slices have miraculously puffed up. It really does look impressive, so I do recommend not putting this in the oven until 30 minutes before you intend to eat it, as you'll want to serve it all puffed up with pride.

Because this is a quick recipe, I didn't make a proper, thickened custard first as the mixture thickens in the oven. Neither did I infuse my cream and milk with a vanilla bean, so I added vanilla paste instead, which has the little, dark seeds you would get from splitting and scraping out the bean. At the last minute, I decided to add a generous slosh of orange extract to the custard, which gave it a heavenly perfume.

SERVES 6

6 Hot Cross Buns
2 Tbsp butter
Handful of chocolate chips (optional)
4 eggs
1½ cups [350 ml] light cream
1½ cups [350 ml] whole milk
2 heaping Tbsp sugar, plus extra for sprinkling
1 tsp ground cinnamon
1 tsp vanilla extract, or 1 heaping tsp vanilla paste
Orange zest, orange extract, candied peel, golden raisins, raisins, currants (use just one, or a combination of these, as you prefer; all are optional)

METHOD

Preheat the oven to 350°F [180°C].

Slice open the Hot Cross Buns and liberally butter each side. Place the halves in a dish just big enough for them all. (If adding chocolate, tuck in some chips around the buns.)

In a bowl mix together the eggs, light cream, and milk. Whisk in the sugar and cinnamon.

Then add the vanilla. If using orange zest, orange extract, candied peel, golden raisins, raisins and/or currants, toss them in now.

Pour the mixture over the buns, and sprinkle over a little extra sugar for crunch. You'll need to squish down the buns into the liquid, to help them soak it all up. Otherwise, they float.

Bake for approximately 30 minutes.

Try not to open the oven door until you think they are ready, as you run the risk of the lovely, puffy pudding collapsing.

Flower Markets

I like little more than a posy of blowsy roses cut from the garden: they can transform a table—see page 155 for some of my tips. If I don't have access to a garden, then a flower market is a truly wonderful thing.

London

Many people don't realize that members of the public can buy from New Covent Garden. You'll be buying wraps—a group of bunches at a time, but often at an advantageous price. (That's the pay-off for getting there at 5 A.M.) Open Monday to Saturday, midnight to 10 A.M. (core trading hours are from 4 A.M.); www.newcoventgardenmarket.com

New York

I head either to Chelsea—the Flower District is around 28th Street between 6th and 7th Avenues—or pick up $10 bunches of roses from the bodegas on every street corner.

Amsterdam

A floating flower market? There's only one in the world: the Bloemenmarkt on Amsterdam's Singel canal. Open Monday to Saturday, 9 A.M. to 5:30 P.M.; Sunday 11 A.M. to 5:30 P.M.; www.iamsterdam.com

BAKED APPLES WITH CINNAMON AND DRIED FRUIT

A baked apple's appeal is all in the light-as-a-cloud fluff of the flesh, mixed with the plump dried fruit and the caramelization of the butter and sugar. Rich, sticky, sinful—and perfect with cold heavy cream.

I often see recipes suggesting that the apples will cook in 25 minutes, but this is a bit optimistic, and if they are those lovely, large ones, you may want to allow at least 40 minutes. The best thing is that they are terribly forgiving, and even if you forget about them, there's nothing not to like about handing out bowls of apple fluff (where they have burst out of their skins.)

The **essential** thing is to make sure you score around their middles with a sharp knife, cutting a good half inch in, as this will stop the apples exploding in the oven. Take it from me: there is nothing enjoyable about scrubbing carbonized apple off the back of the oven.

SERVES 4

4 large apples (I like Rome Beauty or Jonagold)

Heaping ¼ cup [60 g] light brown sugar

¾ cup [100 g] dried fruit (any combination of golden raisins, raisins, currants, candied peel, chopped apricots)

6 Tbsp [80 g] butter, softened

½ tsp ground cinnamon

METHOD

Preheat the oven to 350°F [180°C].

Wash, core, and then score the apples all the way around their middles, ½ in [1 cm] deep.

Brown sugar can get terribly lumpy, so you'll need to push it through a sieve with your fingers, into a bowl. Add the dried fruit, butter, and cinnamon. Using your hands, mash together the ingredients to form a paste. Stuff this into the apple, turning the apples over to check it has gone all the way to the bottom.

Place in an ovenproof dish, and cook for 25 to 40 minutes, depending on the size of the apples.

> ### SECRET
> Buy an apple corer for a few dollars. Your fingers will thank you.

EVE'S PUDDING, THREE WAYS

Eve's pudding—one of my favorite, classic English desserts—is something I first ate at school, where we were often served it doused in custard sauce. Now I prefer it with cream or ice cream, but it's just as good on its own.

Traditionally made from Bramley apples, a tart variety of English apple also known as cookers, it's essentially a hot pound cake with soft, slightly tart apples, which stew underneath as the cake bakes above.

Lots of fruits work in this. I like adding a quince to the apples in the fall; raspberries or blackberries would also be a good addition to apples or peaches.

It can be made in pretty much any kind of ovenproof dish, as it is not turned out at the end of cooking. Don't forget to sprinkle the sugar over the cake mixture before you put it in the oven, to get a lovely, crunchy top.

SERVES 4 TO 6

½ cup [110 g] butter, softened, plus extra for greasing (do NOT use margarine or the baking gods will strike you down)
Approx. 1½ lb [680 g] Granny Smith or Rome Beauty apples
Heaping ½ cup [110 g] sugar, plus extra for sprinkling
2 extra large eggs
1 cup [110 g] self-rising flour
Splash of vanilla extract

METHOD

Preheat the oven to 350°F [180°C] , and generously grease a medium ovenproof dish.

Peel and core the apples. Chop them into large bite-size pieces, and put them in the ovenproof dish.

Cream together the butter and the sugar with a wooden spoon, or in a food processor. I favor the latter. When you're done, it should be light and fluffy.

Add 1 egg, beat. Add a large scoop of flour, beat. Add the second egg, beat. Add the rest of the flour. Add the vanilla extract, beat. It's really that simple.

Spread the mixture over the top of the fruit. Sprinkle with extra sugar and bake for about 25 to 30 minutes.

WITH NECTARINES AND BLUEBERRIES

I first made this version of Eve's pudding for a group of friends when we wanted a very quick, comforting, warm sweet treat after a day of surfing in the cold Cornish sea in southwest England. It was the end of August, and this felt like the perfect cake to straddle the dog days of summer and the beginning of fall: it has both tart and sweet summer fruits, against the comfort of hot cake crumb. You need two nectarines, chopped and pitted, and one cup of blueberries (or enough to fill your chosen oven dish). You could sub peaches for the nectarines, but I prefer nectarines as they keep their shape a bit better. (Peaches do tend to mush quite easily.) Follow the instructions for the apple recipe, opposite, replacing the apples with the nectarines and blueberries.

WITH APRICOTS AND ALMONDS

You will need eight to ten apricots, halved and pitted (or enough to fill your chosen oven dish). Follow the instructions for the apple recipe, opposite, replacing the apples with the apricots and sprinkling with 2 tsp sugar, and replacing ⅓ cup [40 g] of the self-rising flour with ground almonds.

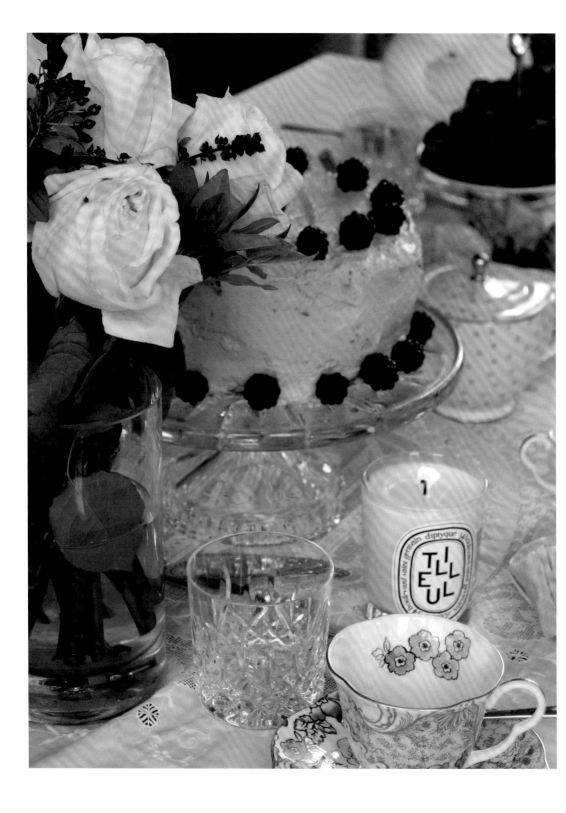

CAKES AND AFTERNOON TEA

Whether I am sitting in a grand-luxe hotel eyeing a stand of teeny-tiny sandwiches, or lolling in front of a fire in the winter at home eating crumpets dripping with butter, afternoon tea will never, ever lose its appeal for me.

Sadly, now that I am older, eating afternoon tea means skipping lunch—and possibly supper, as well. That's because a traditional afternoon tea includes scones, sandwiches, cakes, and cookies. In this chapter I have focused on the cake-and-cookie side of things—I don't think anyone needs a recipe for cucumber or smoked salmon sandwiches. Just remember to season properly, and to cut the crusts off.

The cakes here are split between what I think of as dessert cakes (ones that could be served warm after the entrée, with cream or ice cream) and cold, showstopper cakes (the ones that will impress everyone, but are surprisingly uncomplicated to make).

One thing I have learned from my blog is that although lots of people are horrified at the idea of making a cake from scratch, once they make their first one, they're astonished that it could be so simple. (Cakes were the first thing that I mastered in the kitchen as a little girl.)

I think it's handy to have one cake recipe and one cookie recipe in your repertoire that you can make and adapt at will. The important thing to remember is that baking is a science: you need accurate scales, and don't be tempted to try to freestyle the proportions of butter, sugar, and flour.

However, if you like Herman's Rhubarb Cake (see page 160), there's no reason why you couldn't try it with plums; or if you can't find chocolate wafer truffles for the Milk Chocolate Layer Cake (see page 149), use your favorite equivalent instead. The key is to play with the flavorings, not the building blocks.

The single most important thing to learn in cake-making is not to overmix the mixture once the flour has been added—this will overstretch the gluten in the flour and give you a leaden, heavy cake.

TRIPLE-LAYER LEMON CAKE
WITH FRESH BLACKBERRY JAM AND BLACKBERRY SWISS MERINGUE BUTTERCREAM

This cake is my showstopper: it has never, ever failed me, and never, ever fails to impress. I think everyone needs one cake that they can wheel out for special occasions, and once you have mastered this, you will always have the perfect cake for any occasion in your repertoire.

It's based on a British classic—Victoria sponge cake—which holds up perfectly. Because I am not great at splitting cakes with a knife, I bake three layers to sandwich together. The frosting is a light and fluffy, delectably smooth, meringue-based dream.

SERVES 12 GENEROUSLY

1 quantity Fresh Blackberry Jam (page 146)
1 quantity Swiss Meringue Buttercream (page 146), flavored with juice from the Fresh Blackberry Jam
Small basket blackberries

For the Victoria sponge cake
3 cups + 1 Tbsp [375 g] all-purpose flour
2 tsp baking powder
1½ cups + 3 Tbsp [375 g] butter, softened
1¾ cups + 2 Tbsp [375 g] granulated sugar
Grated zest of 2 lemons
6 eggs
3 x 8-in [20-cm] round cake pans, greased and lined with baking parchment

---

SECRET
It's best to buy springform, loose-bottomed cake pans, as there is less chance of the cake mixture sticking to the pan.

METHOD

For the Victoria sponge cake, preheat the oven to 350°F [180°C]. Sift the flour and baking powder into a bowl.

Put the butter, sugar, and lemon zest into a large mixing bowl, and beat using a wooden spoon or a mixer with a paddle attachment until light and fluffy. Add 1 egg at a time, along with a spoonful of flour to the butter mixture to prevent the mixture curdling. Add the rest of the flour, a big spoonful at a time, being careful to stop beating the moment the flour is incorporated. (Overbeating leads to a heavier cake.) Divide the mixture equally between the cake pans and bake for 25 to 30 minutes. Allow the cakes to cool for 10 minutes before turning them out of the pans, and allowing them to cool completely on wire racks.

Spoon half the Fresh Blackberry Jam over one layer of cake to form the bottom, being careful to gently squish the blackberries into the cake. (This allows for a pretty effect when the cake is cut.) Repeat on a second layer. Take the Swiss Meringue Buttercream, put a dollop on the bottom layer, and carefully spread out from the middle with a knife over all the jam. Resist the temptation to use too much, as it will just squirt out of the sides. Carefully place the next jam-covered layer of cake on top, and repeat the buttercream process.

Then add the final layer of cake. Smooth the remainder of the buttercream on the top and around the sides, paying special attention to the gaps between the layers, which you should fill in with extra frosting. Decorate with blackberries.

SWISS MERINGUE BUTTERCREAM

SMB is lighter than normal buttercream, and is consequently much easier to spread. It calls for a weight of egg whites, as egg sizes are imprecise. I've had great success using cartons of pasteurized egg whites, but if you use whole eggs, remember that yolks freeze (don't forget to write the quantity on the container).

You will need both a handheld electric whisk and a stand mixer to make this frosting along with a cooking thermometer. I strongly suggest investing in a digital one.

MAKES PLENTY FOR A TRIPLE-LAYER CAKE
12 oz [340 g] egg whites (approx. 11 to 12 eggs)
3 cups + 2¼ Tbsp [625 g] granulated sugar
2¾ cups + 1 Tbsp [625 g] soft butter, cut into
    pieces
1 Tbsp vanilla extract
3 Tbsp juice from Fresh Blackberry Jam
    (see right), to color the buttercream

METHOD
Place a large saucepan over medium heat and quarter-fill with water, placing the metal bowl from a stand mixer over the water in the pan. Alternatively, use a heatproof bowl. Pour in the egg whites and sugar and start beating together with a handheld electric whisk. Place the thermometer in the mixture and beat constantly until it reaches 140°F [60°C]. This will take at least 10 minutes. Now remove the metal bowl from the pan to the stand mixer and beat on high until it is glossy and peaked, and both the meringue and bowl are completely cool (about 10 minutes).

Swap the beater attachment for the whisk and start adding the butter pieces with the motor still running. When it is all incorporated, add the vanilla extract and juice and beat for 5 minutes.

Very occasionally, SMB curdles in the mixer. Don't cry: there is a simple rescue. Remove 4 heaping spoonfuls and microwave on high for 15 seconds. Place back in the mixer bowl and beat again, gradually increasing the speed, until smooth again.

FRESH BLACKBERRY JAM

I love a fruit layer in pound cakes, but I am not so keen on using jam: I find it too sweet, too heavy, and too sticky. This recipe came about when I was trying to find an alternative to jam that was thicker than a compote, so it wouldn't run off the cake, but not so dense that it wouldn't spread. (A recipe in US *Country Living* magazine was the starting point for this idea.) It's essentially berries, made to give up their juices by the addition of a little sugar and heat, and thickened with cornstarch.

MAKES APPROX. 1 JAM JAR
2¾ cups [375 g] fresh or frozen blackberries
1 Tbsp crème de mûre, or any
    fruit liqueur (optional)
⅓ cup [70 g] granulated sugar
1 Tbsp fresh lemon juice
1 Tbsp cornstarch
2 Tbsp water

METHOD
Place the blackberries, fruit liqueur, if using, sugar, and lemon juice in a saucepan and heat very gently until the blackberries begin to soften and give up their juice.

Using a slotted spoon, remove the blackberries to a bowl and squash them gently with the back of a spoon. Set a sieve over the saucepan and strain the juice back in. Set the strained berries aside.

Sift the cornstarch into a small bowl (this is important or you will get lumps), and add the 2 Tbsp water, stirring briskly with a teaspoon or mini whisk to ensure the water and cornstarch are wholly combined.

Put the mixture into the berry juice, stir, and bring to a boil. Lower the heat, and simmer until the mixture is thick and jam-like. Pour in the reserved blackberries, stir, and then pour the jam into a clean bowl to cool.

If using in a cake, make sure it is completely cool first. It will keep for 2 to 3 days in the fridge.

VANILLA CUPCAKES
WITH FRESH RASPBERRIES AND RASPBERRY FROSTING

I think food that has a surprise inside is always beguiling, and these pale pink, raspberry-flecked, frosted cupcakes look like the simplest cakes on the tea table. But when you cut them in half, there's a fresh raspberry lurking in the middle, giving a lovely sharp contrast to the decadently creamy frosting.

MAKES 8 TO 10

½ cup [110 g] butter, softened
Heaping ½ cup [110 g]
  granulated sugar
2 eggs
1 tsp vanilla extract
½ cup + 2 Tbsp [80 g]
  self-rising flour, sifted
⅓ cup [30 g] ground almonds
24 raspberries

For the frosting
9 Tbsp [125 g] butter, softened
1⅔ cups [250 g] powdered
  sugar
1 Tbsp milk
2 tsp raspberry jam
8 raspberries
12-hole cupcake pan, lined with
paper cupcake cases

METHOD

Preheat the oven to 350°F [180°C].

Cream together the butter and the sugar using a wooden spoon or a mixer with a paddle attachment until light and fluffy. Beat in the eggs and vanilla extract.

Mix together the flour and ground almonds in a separate bowl. Now fold into the egg mixture.

Divide the mixture between 8 to 10 cupcake cases (I use a small ice cream scoop). Bake for 15 to 20 minutes, or until risen and golden.

Tip the baked cupcakes out of the pan and allow to cool completely on a wire rack.

For the frosting, put the butter in a large mixing bowl. Sift the powdered sugar into the bowl, a little at a time, beating it into the butter until smooth. Then, beat in the milk and raspberry jam. Squash the raspberries with the back of a fork, then beat into the frosting until evenly incorporated.

Using a small, very sharp knife, scoop out a raspberry-sized hole in the top of each fairy cake. Insert a raspberry.

The frosting can either be piped on in swirls, using a piping bag, or smoothed on with the flat of a knife. Top with another raspberry.

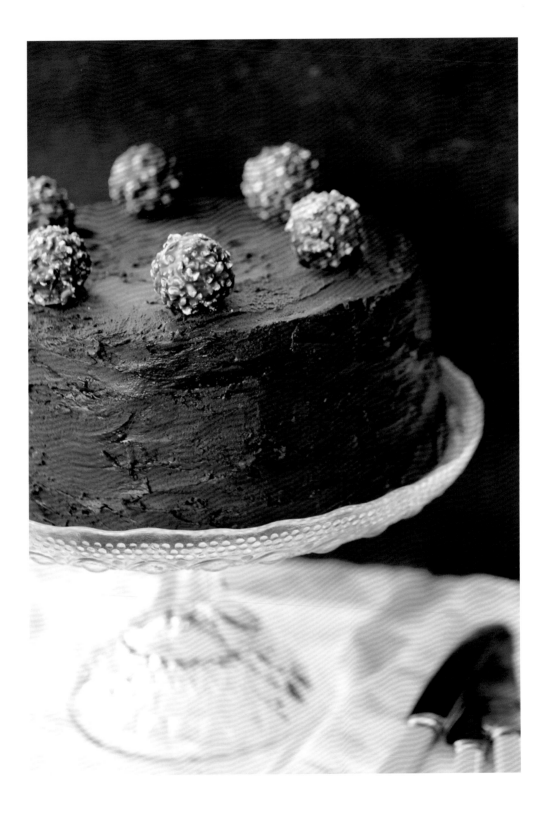

MILK CHOCOLATE LAYER CAKE

This is my slightly more adult riff on the first chocolate cake I can remember eating, which was billed as a milk chocolate cake because it used hot cocoa mix in the cake mixture, as opposed to proper, grown-up chocolate. This makes it great for children, as it's not at all rich, but because it has a proper chocolate frosting, it still delivers that delicious theobromine hit. The evaporated milk is a clever touch because it makes for a deliciously light and moist crumb.

SERVES 10 TO 12

3 cups + 2 Tbsp [375 g] self-rising flour
4 Tbsp hot cocoa mix
6 Tbsp cocoa powder
2¼ cups [450 g] granulated sugar
½ tsp salt
¾ cup + 2 Tbsp [200 g] butter
4 eggs
5 Tbsp evaporated milk
5 Tbsp water
2 tsp vanilla extract

For the chocolate fudge frosting
16 chocolate wafer truffles (I use Ferrero Rocher)
¾ cup [175 g] butter
8 Tbsp cocoa powder, sifted
8 Tbsp evaporated milk
2 tsp vanilla extract
3 cups [600 g] powdered sugar
Two deep, 8-in [20-cm] round springform or loose-bottomed cake pans, greased

SECRET
If you have stupendous self-control, this cake not only keeps very well, but it travels perfectly, as the fudge frosting is quite firm.

METHOD
Preheat the oven to 350°F [180°C].

Put the dry ingredients and the butter in a food processor and whizz together. You can make this in a stand mixer, but the processor makes for a smoother mixture.

Mix together all the liquid ingredients, then add to the processor. Whizz together until the mixture is well-combined, but be careful not to overbeat as this will result in a heavy cake. Divide the mixture between the greased cake pans, smoothing off the top.

Bake for about 35 to 45 minutes. The cake should be springy when pressed with a finger, and a toothpick inserted in the middle will come out clean. Turn out carefully onto a wire rack, and allow to cool for at least 1 hour before frosting.

For the chocolate fudge frosting, smash up 10 of the chocolate wafer truffles and set aside. Put the butter in a saucepan over very low heat, and add the cocoa. Whisk together as the butter melts.

Combine the evaporated milk and vanilla extract in either a stand mixer, or a large mixing bowl. Remove the cocoa and butter from the heat, add to the milk mixture, and beat well. Sift in the powdered sugar gradually (do not skip the sifting or you will end up with lumpy frosting) and beat very well in either the mixer, or with a wooden spoon until smooth. Do not add all the sugar at once as the frosting becomes impossible to stir. Once mixed, use immediately as it hardens quickly.

In a small bowl place 2 generous tablespoons of the frosting and mix with the smashed chocolates. Dollop the mixture on top of one cake layer, spread it out evenly, and then sandwich with the second cake layer. Frost the top with the remaining frosting, smoothing with a spatula down towards the side. Then frost the sides. Dipping the spatula in water will help smooth the frosting. Decorate the top immediately with the 6 remaining chocolate wafer truffles.

BROWNIES

If I had to name a signature bake, this would be it. I've made these brownies in kitchens all over the world, for friends and for enemies. There are very few people who can resist the lure of these gooey, intensely chocolatey squares.

Best of all, they take less than ten minutes to prepare, so are a great last-minute gift or treat. I sometimes serve them warm as a dessert with chocolate sauce and ice cream, and chopped up small, they are a vital part of my Hot Brownie Sundae (see page 186) and Individual Chocolate Trifles (see page 129).

Note that cake-release spray, available online and in some supermarkets and cookshops, is a godsend for making brownies, as the nuts can often stick to the sides of the cake pan. Otherwise make sure you thoroughly line the pan with parchment paper, or a silicone baking sheet.

MAKES 8 TO 10

6 oz [175 g] bittersweet chocolate (I like 70% cocoa solids)

¾ cup [175 g] butter

3 eggs

1 cup [200 g] superfine or granulated sugar

1 tsp vanilla extract

1¼ cups [150 g] chopped walnuts

1 cup [110 g] all-purpose flour, sifted

Pinch of salt

8-in [20-cm] square baking pan, greased or lined with parchment paper

SECRET

If you want a truly luxurious treat, plop a teaspoon of hazelnut chocolate spread at regular intervals into the mixture once in the pan.

METHOD

Melt the chocolate and the butter together in a heavy saucepan over very low heat. If you are nervous about the chocolate burning (or if the pan is lightweight), simply pour boiling water into the pan and place a heatproof bowl—such as Pyrex—over the water so that it fits without touching the water. Put the chocolate and butter in the bowl and allow to melt.

When the chocolate and butter have melted, remove from the heat and allow to cool for about 5 to 10 minutes. This is so the eggs do not scramble when they are added to the hot mixture.

Beat together the eggs, sugar, and vanilla extract. Add the melted chocolate and butter mixture to the eggs and beat. Then add the walnuts, flour, and salt. Make sure everything is thoroughly mixed together, as the flour has a habit of forming bubbles.

Pour the mixture into the prepared pan and bake for approximately 20 to 25 minutes. They should still be gooey in the middle. Remove the pan from the oven, and allow the brownies to cool in the pan.

Tip the brownies out onto a board and cut into 8 to 10 portions.

PLUM AND ALMOND LITTLE CAKES

These are made in a traditional muffin pan without paper muffin cases. This results in lovely miniature cakes, as opposed to cupcake shapes. I recommend a silicone muffin pan here, but if you don't have one, use either butter, or cake release spray to thoroughly grease the holes of the pan.

MAKES 12

11 Tbsp [150 g] butter
½ cup [100 g] superfine or
  granulated sugar, plus extra
  for sprinkling
¼ cup [50 g] light brown sugar
3 eggs
1 tsp almond extract
¾ cup [100 g] self-rising flour,
  sifted
1 tsp baking powder
½ cup [50 g] ground almonds
2 plums, pitted and chopped
12-hole muffin pan (silicone is
  best here)

METHOD
Preheat the oven to 350°F [180°C].

Cream together the butter and both sugars using a wooden spoon or a mixer with a paddle attachment until light and fluffy. Add the eggs and almond extract, followed by the flour, baking powder, and ground almonds.

Then, using a metal spoon, fold in the chopped plums.

Divide the mixture between the 12 holes of the muffin pan (I use a small ice cream scoop).

Sprinkle a little granulated sugar over the top of each cake. Bake for 15 to 20 minutes, or until risen and golden.

Take the little cakes out of the pan and allow to cool on a wire rack.

CHOCOLATE CHUNK COOKIES

I am obsessed with baking the perfect chocolate chip cookie. This is partly because, historically, cookies have not been an area where I shine, but also because I want a go-to cookie recipe that I can knock up in under half an hour, with no dough resting overnight in the fridge, or special measures required.

I like to use bars of 70 percent chocolate as opposed to chocolate chips. I chop them up myself with a large knife, which gives lots of tiny scrapings and creates an attractively striated effect when baked. Because I use chocolate with a higher proportion of cocoa solids, the cookies are slightly less sweet than you may expect. What's more, they are not delicate, friable cookies, or those bendy, almost-raw-in-the-middle cookies of shopping malls; nor are they parsimonious with the chocolate. What they are is a beguiling combination of crisp, thick and chewy.

MAKES APPROX. 20

9 oz [250 g] dark chocolate
Heaping ¾ cup [175 g] granulated sugar
¼ cup [50 g] light brown sugar
11 Tbsp [150 g] butter, softened
2 tsp vanilla extract
1 whole egg, fridge-cold
1 egg yolk, fridge-cold
2½ cups [300 g] all-purpose flour
½ tsp baking powder
3 baking sheets lined with parchment paper or silicone baking sheets, or just greased

METHOD

Preheat the oven to 350°F [180°C].

Break up the chocolate into pieces, then take a large knife, and using a rocking action, chop into little chunks. (To do this, place one hand flat on top of the knife tip, and one curved around the handle as normal.) Make sure you reserve all the little scrapings.

Pour both sugars into a mixing bowl. Mash out any lumps in the brown sugar with a fork. Add the butter, and cream together using a wooden spoon or a mixer with a paddle attachment until light and fluffy. Add the vanilla extract and eggs, and beat again thoroughly.

Sift in the flour and baking powder: it will seem like a lot, but don't worry. Beat everything together, but be very careful not to overmix. Carefully stir in the chocolate by hand, making sure it is evenly distributed through the dough.

This is a nice, thick dough. Use either a small ice cream scoop for super-even cookies, or just scoop up small balls with a spoon.

Gently flatten them out on the baking sheets, so they look like hockey pucks, and lay them out in 2 long rows per sheet leaving plenty of room for the cookies to spread out. Six should fit on a standard, rectangular sheet.

Bake for about 15 minutes. They will go quite golden because of the sugars, and will be a little floppy in the middle from the melted chocolate, so leave them to cool on the baking sheets for 5 minutes, then carefully lift with a spatula to a wire rack to cool.

POMEGRANATE MOLASSES SPICE COOKIES

Molasses cookies (made from molasses, or treacle) are a classic American recipe, and I developed mine after tasting a memorable version on a road trip through central California.

As for pomegranate molasses, it's extraordinary how many people now have a bottle of this lurking in a kitchen cupboard, which comes out maybe once a month. I like it drizzled over halloumi cheese for a quick lunch, and it's an integral part of my roast cauliflower salad, but the huge bottle is still sitting there half-full and sticky. When I came back to England I wondered what would happen if I added pomegranate molasses to my standard molasses cookie recipe. It was a great success: the pomegranate cuts the sweetness and enhances the spice.

I use baking soda rather than baking powder in this recipe, as molasses is a reagent for baking soda (it gets rid of the bitter taste), but it does mean you need to bake the cookie dough immediately, as the reaction starts in the mixing bowl.

MAKES APPROX. 15

9 Tbsp [120 g] butter, softened
Scant ¼ cup [70 g] molasses
⅓ cup [70 g] light brown sugar
Scant ⅓ cup [60 g] granulated
  sugar
1 egg
2½ Tbsp pomegranate molasses
2¼ cups [275 g] all-purpose flour
2 tsp baking soda
1 tsp ground cinnamon
2 tsp ground allspice
1½ tsp ground ginger
2 to 3 baking sheets lined with
  parchment paper or silicone
  baking sheets, or just greased

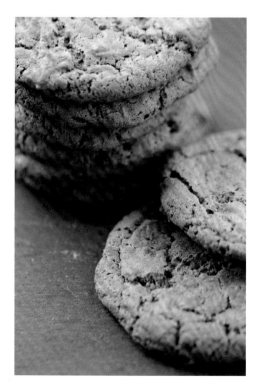

METHOD
Preheat the oven to 350°F [180°C].

Cream together the butter, molasses, and both sugars. (This is best done in a food processor, as the sugars are very dense.)

Beat the egg and pomegranate molasses together, and add to the butter and sugar mixture, mixing in well.

Sift together the flour, baking soda, and spices, and add to the bowl, being careful not to overmix.

Use your hands to create balls of dough about the size of a chocolate truffle, and place them on the baking sheets, but do not press each ball down. Leave plenty of room for them to spread out, and count on fitting about 6 on a standard baking sheet.

Bake for 20 to 25 minutes. The cookies are done when they are crisp around the edges, but still slightly soft in the middle—they will harden as they cool, so be careful lifting them off the baking sheet.

NUTTY CHOCOLATE PALMIERS

I take a great deal of pleasure in baking boxes and boxes full of cakes, muffins, cookies, fudge, and other candy to deliver as thank-you Christmas presents. Amongst them are always these palmiers, which are a cinch to make and are fun to do with children too, as all they involve is a bit of pastry rolling and some Nutella spreading.

They are especially good eaten warm (not piping hot) from the oven, as the flaky pastry showers over your clothes as you bite into them, and the warm Nutella and butter drips down your wrist.

MAKES APPROX. 26

Flour, for dusting

Approx. 14 oz [375 g] ready-made puff pastry sheets

²/₃ cup [140 g] hazelnut chocolate spread (Nutella can't be beaten)

½ cup [60 g] chopped, toasted nuts (hazelnuts, pecans, almonds, peanuts are all good)

1 egg, lightly beaten

Granulated sugar, for sprinkling

1 to 2 baking sheets lined with parchment paper or silicone baking sheets, or just greased

METHOD

Preheat the oven to 350°F [180°C].

Sprinkle some flour over a work surface and lay out the pastry sheets. Roll out once with a rolling pin, in one direction. (It doesn't rise properly if you mess it about too much.) If rolling out a square of pastry, roll it to a thickness of about ¼ in [0.5 cm].

Scoop the hazelnut chocolate spread out into a bowl and heat it gently in a bain-marie, or a bowl set over a pan of simmering water, until it loosens. Be careful not to overheat, as it can separate. (The packaging specifically warns against microwaving.)

Take a knife, dip it in the bain-marie or saucepan of boiling water, and then dip it into the spread. Spread the chocolate all over the flattened pastry, then scatter the chopped nuts all over the top. Now roll up each long side towards the middle until they meet.

Using a very sharp knife, cut the roll into ⁵/₈-in [1.5-cm] slices. Use the flat of a cook's knife to gently squash them flat.

Set the palmiers out on the baking sheets, giving them enough room to spread during baking—you should be able to fit 4 across. Brush each palmier with beaten egg and sprinkle sugar over the top.

Bake for 25 minutes for the palmiers to turn a light, golden brown, but check at 20. Using a spatula (the chocolate spread gets boiling hot so use fingers at your peril), lift them off the baking sheets onto a wire rack to cool down.

If one palmier needs to be tested for deliciousness immediately, do watch out for the very hot chocolate spread. And do wait until the palmiers are completely cool before putting them into a tin, otherwise they will go soggy.

FLOWERS FOR THE KITCHEN TABLE

It's a wonderful indulgence to have flowers on my kitchen table when friends come around to eat. Of course, I don't have time to create lavish arrangements, but a few tricks can transform a bunch or two of inexpensive flowers into something rather impressive.

I always keep odd-shaped glass jars once they are empty, along with medicine bottles, small jam jars, and the glasses from scented candles, as they all make great vases.

The quickest trick is to tie a piece of string loosely under the heads of a single bunch of roses and chop off the stems quite short, to the height of the (small-ish) vase you wish to place them in. This will give a wonderful massed effect. Do make sure the vase you choose isn't too tall—about 6 in [15 cm] is perfect.

After the liquid has evaporated from the little square or round glass vessels that are used as scent diffusers, I wash the bottles and use a cluster of three or five (always odd numbers) as tiny vases, clustered together. A single rose; a stalk of veronica; maybe a piece of eucalyptus and a piece of scented stock; or an open ranunculus or anemone: a stem in each vase, cut at different heights, always looks charming.

If you use jam jars as vases, a handy trick is to think in thirds: the height of the flowers sticking out of the top of the jam jar should be twice the height of the jar.

ICE CREAM BIRTHDAY CAKE

My sister Holly's birthday falls in the middle of August, and for all the years of our childhood, our mother made an ice cream birthday cake adapted from a Delia Smith recipe, for her party. (That's Holly and our mother Victoria in the photo to the right with this very cake.)

It's a super-light whisked cake, split and layered with vanilla ice cream. The sides are held together with sugary ladyfingers painted with apricot jam to stick them onto the sides of the cake; semi-set gelatin is poured over the top, and the whole lot bunged in the freezer to settle and firm up. (Believe me, frozen gelatin is delicious.)

Of course we had our own family twist on it. One year we had no strawberry gelatin for the frozen top, so my mother used lime green. Although we all preferred pink gelatin, the radioactive look became a family tradition.

SERVES 10 TO 12

For the whisked cake
1²/₃ cups [200 g] self-rising flour, plus extra for dusting
8 eggs
1 cup [200 g] granulated sugar
1 tsp baking powder

For the filling and topping
1½ quarts [1.5 L] vanilla ice cream
4-oz package pink jello dessert
2 Tbsp seedless jam (apricot is good)
1½ packages (approx. 30) ladyfingers
Two deep, 8-in [20-cm] round springform or loose-bottomed cake pans, greased
One very deep, 8-in [20-cm] round cake pan (preferably springform), sides and base lined with parchment paper
Ribbon, to tie around the middle

METHOD

For the whisked cake, preheat the oven to 350°F [180°C]. Toss a teaspoon of extra flour into each of the two greased cake pans and shake them about to coat the insides evenly in flour.

Put the eggs and sugar into a large mixing bowl, and whisk with a handheld electric whisk until very thick and pale. When you can lift the beaters and leave a thin ribbon trail sitting on the mixture, it is ready. This will take 5 to 10 minutes depending on the freshness of the eggs.

Sift together the flour and baking powder, then carefully fold them into the egg mixture using a metal spoon. Be careful not to overmix it, as you need as much air as possible to allow the cake to rise.

Divide the mixture equally between the prepared cake pans and bake for 25 to 30 minutes. A toothpick inserted in the middle should come out clean. Run a knife around the insides of the pans and turn out onto a wire rack. The cakes must be completely cooled before you decorate them—this takes around 1 hour.

Take the ice cream out of the freezer about 20 minutes before you need it, to allow to soften slightly.

When the cakes are cool, check them to see how level they are and, if necessary, use a serrated knife carefully to flatten the tops. Choose the neater cake for the top layer. Carefully slice each cake layer in half horizontally to give 4 layers of cake in total.

Now fit one cake layer into the base of the deep, lined cake pan and spoon one-third of the ice cream over it, spreading it out evenly. Place another cake layer on top of the ice cream, followed by another third of ice cream, the third layer of cake, and the final third of ice cream. Top with the fourth cake layer.

Tightly cover the top of the cake pan with foil and freeze the cake overnight. (You can leave it for several days in the freezer.)

The morning of the day on which you wish to serve the cake, make the pink jello dessert in a shallow bowl, dissolving it in 1 cup [275 ml] **only** of hot water. (Ignore the package instructions.)

Remove the cake from the freezer, take off the foil, and slowly and carefully spoon the gelatin all over the surface, where it will start to set almost immediately because of the ice-cold cake. Don't worry if any gelatin makes a break for freedom; it won't show once the sides of the cake are covered with ladyfingers.

Cover the cake with the foil once again, and return to the freezer for at least 1 hour. (You can store it in this state for up to a month, although my patience has never lasted this long.)

Take the cake out of the freezer at least 1 hour before serving. Meanwhile, gently warm the jam in a small saucepan.

Hold a hot, damp dishcloth round the pan for a few seconds, then ease the cake gently upwards from the pan ring by pushing on the loose base. Slide a spatula underneath between the cake and the pan base, and transfer the cake onto a plate.

Now spread the plain sides of the ladyfingers with the warm jam and position them vertically all around the side of the cake.

Use the ribbon to hold the ladyfingers in place as you position them. (You may find a few pins helpful here.) Keep in the fridge until needed.

Wonderful Places to Drink Tea and Eat Cake

NEW YORK: Cha-An

A few blocks from my first apartment in the East Village, Cha-An does an afternoon tea that's both delicious and inexpensive. It's also unexpected: this is a Japanese tea house and their decidedly untraditional take includes matcha shortbread, Earl-Grey scones, and ten types of green tea.

230 East 9th Street, New York, NY 10003; www.chaanteahouse.com

LONDON: The Modern Pantry

Any of the grand London hotels like The Connaught, Claridge's, or The Dorchester will serve an immaculate afternoon tea, with much white-glove ritual, but I also like the low-key, traditional charm of The Goring (hard by Buckingham Palace), or the leftfield take of The Modern Pantry in Clerkenwell, where the chocolate mousse cake is spiked with chili and licorice, and the dacquoise is made with green tea and toasted, black sesame seeds.

The Modern Pantry, 47–48 St John's Square, London EC1V 4JJ; www.themodernpantry.co.uk

BERLIN: Barcomi's Deli and Café

I first visited Barcomi's—hidden off a charming, secret courtyard—when I was directed there by a flurry of recommendations on Twitter. There is a huge display case full of the most delicious cakes: those showing restraint can order a single slice. Others (ahem, myself) can order a tasting plate with a slice from four different cakes. (The cheesecake is as if made by angels.)

Sophienstraße 21, 10178 Berlin; www.barcomis.de

SAN FRANCISCO: Japanese Tea Garden

This beautiful tea garden, inside San Francisco's Golden Gate Park, has long been one of my favorite places to sit and serenely contemplate my navel. When I am not feeling so introspective, I eat dorayaki (pancakes filled with red bean paste) and watch the Japanese tea ceremony demonstrations inside the authentic tea house. The best time to visit is in March and April when the cherry blossoms bloom.

75 Hagiwara Tea Garden Drive, San Francisco CA 94118; www.japaneseteagardensf.com

HERMAN'S RHUBARB CAKE
WITH CRUMBLE TOPPING

I spend a few weeks each summer at the French home of Herman, the father of a dear old school friend. It's a farmhouse set in the middle of fields, and the shops are an energetic bike ride away. I bake endless cakes for the legions of family who appear without warning, so imagine my joy on discovering copious rhubarb patches all around the house. I take enormous pleasure in wandering out into the intense August heat, armed with an ancient wooden-handled knife, and kneeling in the grass to cut the rhubarb stalks. I trim them then and there, tossing the umbrella leaves into the compost bin under the kitchen window.

This is the perfect cake for feeding a big, hungry family; it serves ten as a warm dessert cake, with custard sauce. It always goes down amazingly well: the French cake-eating record is three slices down one gullet at one sitting.

It's also quick to make: with a food processor it can be done in 15 minutes. It does take a while to bake, though: depending on your oven, you need to allow up to an hour and a half for it to bake through.

For this cake, it's better to go for a wide pan than a deeper one if you have a choice, as it will take far too long to bake otherwise, and you risk a dark brown outside and molten middle. (I once made this cake in a pan so wide that my batter was only 2 in [5 cm] high, and it still tasted delicious.)

SERVES 10

Generous 1¾ cups [400 g]
   butter, softened
2 cups [400 g] granulated sugar
6 eggs
3¼ cups + 1 Tbsp [400 g]
   self-rising flour
3½ cups [500 g] chopped
   rhubarb, tossed with
   1 Tbsp sugar

For the crumble topping
11 Tbsp [150 g] fridge-cold
   butter, cut into cubes
1¼ cups [150 g] all-purpose
   flour
2½ Tbsp [30 g] granulated
   sugar
10-in [25-cm] springform or
   loose-bottomed cake pan,
   greased, and base and sides
   lined with parchment paper

METHOD

Preheat the oven to 350°F [180°C].

In a food processor (or with a handheld electric whisk), cream together the butter and sugar until light and fluffy. Beat 3 eggs, and add to the mixture. Whizz together. Add 4 Tbsp of the flour. Whizz. Add the last 3 eggs, beaten together. Whizz. Add the rest of the flour. Whizz. That's your cake mixture. Pour it into the cake pan. Scatter over the chopped rhubarb. (Don't mix it in, as it would all sink to the bottom. This way it distributes itself evenly through the cake as it cooks.)

For the crumble topping, pulse together the butter and flour in a food processor, or mix with your fingertips. Think crumbs, rather than a ball. Pour the crumbs over the rhubarb, and sprinkle over the sugar.

Bake for about 1 hour 30 minutes. After 30 minutes, turn the oven down to about 325°F [160°C], so that the outside doesn't get too crispy while the middle bakes. If you think the top is browning too quickly, place a piece of parchment paper over the top. The cake is baked when a knife inserted in the middle comes out clean. (Make sure you don't pierce a piece of fruit, as this will give a false positive.) The crumble topping will not color very much, so do not use this as a guide for done-ness.

MY FAVORITE SPARKLING WINES

Laurent-Perrier Cuvée Rosé
My favorite pink Champagne (I drank it to celebrate writing this book).

Bollinger Special Cuvée
Full-bodied and gently sparkling, this is a very grown-up wine.

Nyetimber Classic Cuvée 2009
This sparkling wine from a vineyard in the South Downs is a wonderful way to celebrate British winemaking.

PARTIES

I used to get into a tizzy when the prospect of entertaining more than a few people loomed. It took me several years of self-flagellation before I understood that people just want to feel looked after at a party, so I stopped trying to impress with fiddly canapés or complicated menus for 20, and concentrated more on doing one or two things properly. (As well as making sure there was plenty of space for coats, lots of ice, soft drinks, and toilet paper, and a cracking party playlist.)

In this chapter you'll find my tried-and-tested plan for a cocktail party—where the food on offer is chicken pie and a pile of brownies—plenty of suggestions for simple party food to serve lots of people, much of which can be prepped in advance, and my top tips for party-throwing.

Balancing the requirements of guests, food, and drink can be tricky, which is why planning everything in advance is the most important part of your organization. You'll be surprised how much calmer you'll be when the event finally rolls around.

I've also included some of my favorite interactive meals in this chapter—and by that I mean big dishes of food into which everyone can dive, and recipes that get everyone involved in making up their own food: think Bang Bang Chicken (page 179) or DIY Salmon and Vegetable Parcels with Lemon Cream Sauce (page 182). They involve a bit of prep, but their genius is that the host or hostess isn't chained to the kitchen.

PARTY TIPS

- Fill the bath with ice and water as a temporary ice bucket
- You will always need more ice than you think
- Start chiling the wine and Champagne the day before
- Ban red wine
- Have empty cardboard boxes stashed away for all the empties
- Buy extra corkscrews if you are serving wine: – someone WILL lose the only one
- Don't serve anything with tomato in: spills never come out
- Avoid candles: conflagrations are not chic
- Prime the neighbors
- Make sure you have enough cash to pay helpers
- And for the biggest party luxury: book your cleaning lady for the next morning

FIVE COCKTAILS IN PITCHERS

As a guide, I usually estimate a generous ¼ cup [50 ml] alcohol per head for a mixed cocktail. Most standard-sized glass pitchers have a capacity of between 5 and 6½ cups [1.25 and 1.5 L]. Recipes below fill one cocktail pitcher, serving five to six, depending on how much ice you use. Note: "muddling" means to crush together herbs and sugar using a "muddler" or spoon to release the aromatic oils.

LEMON, THYME, AND VODKA

This cocktail is shaken not stirred, so you'll need to make a couple of batches to fill your pitcher. (The shaking is important as it bruises the herb, and infuses its natural oil into the vodka.)

2 sprigs of fresh thyme, plus extra to garnish
¾ cup [175 ml] vodka (or lemon vodka if you have it)
Ice cubes
⅓ cup [75 ml] Limoncello
⅓ cup [75 ml] lemon juice
Sparkling or soda water

Pick off the thyme leaves and add with the vodka to a cocktail shaker. Add a few cubes of ice, and make like Tom Cruise for a minute or so. Strain into a pitcher, and add the Limoncello and lemon juice. Top up with sparkling or soda water. Serve in a highball. Garnish with a thyme sprig.

ELDERFLOWER, MINT, GIN, AND CUCUMBER

Ice cubes
1 cup [250 ml] gin
¾ cup [175 ml] elderflower syrup
1 cucumber, sliced
Large handful mint leaves
Sparkling or soda water

Place a handful of ice into a pitcher and pour over the gin and elderflower syrup. Add the cucumber and mint, and top up with sparkling water. Stir vigorously. Serve in a highball.

RASPBERRY MARTINIS

4 cups [600 g] canned raspberries in syrup (not natural juice)
¼ cup [50 ml] Chambord or crème de framboise
Generous ¾ cup [200 ml] vodka, ideally from the freezer
Ice cubes

Tip the raspberries and their syrup into a blender and whizz. Mix the Chambord or crème de framboise with the chilled vodka and raspberry juice. Fill one-third of a glass pitcher with ice cubes, pour in the cocktail, and strain into a Martini glass.

A NOD TO AN "OLD-FASHIONED": WHISKEY AND BITTERS

¼ cup [50 g] granulated sugar
10 dashes Angostura Bitters
1 cup [250 ml] whiskey
⅓ cup [75 ml] orange juice (e.g. blood orange)
Ice cubes
Orange zest strips and 1 maraschino cherry per cocktail, to garnish

Muddle together the sugar and bitters, then add the whiskey and orange juice and stir. Fill one-third of a pitcher with ice cubes, then pour in the cocktail. Serve immediately, strained into a tumbler. Garnish with the zest and cherry.

PINK WHIPPET (NAMED IN HONOR OF MY MOTHER'S WHIPPET, BILLY)

Scant 2 Tbsp [25 g] granulated sugar
1 large handful mint leaves, plus extra to garnish
4½ cups [1 L] pink grapefruit juice
1 cup [250 ml] vodka
Ice cubes

Muddle together the sugar, mint leaves, and grapefruit juice, then add the vodka. Fill one-third of a pitcher with ice cubes, then pour in the cocktail. Serve immediately, strained into a martini glass and garnished with mint.

BUTTERNUT SQUASH PUREE FOR SKEPTICS

When I moved to the US, I was amazed at the prevalence of dips, especially quite substantial ones. (In the UK they are always quite liquid.) One of the things I really like about American parties at home are the wonderful, big bowls of dips that friends bring over for gatherings both large and small, whether or not they've been asked to bring food.

In New York or San Francisco, it was perfectly normal for a girlfriend to rock up to my front door for a TV party with a snazzy, multi-layered dip—almost a meal in itself, and made according to a honed family recipe.

There certainly isn't a UK equivalent of this particularly US tradition, and you won't find them in very many British cookbooks. They just aren't taken that seriously here; most often they lurk in tiny plastic pots in the chiller section of the supermarket.

The first thing to acknowledge about the whole dippage thing, is that they are very rarely bursting with goodness—unless your view of goodness is all about sour cream, cheese, and a zillion calories, in which case your luck is so in.

The second is that dips aren't just something delicious whizzed up in the food processor in seconds (although that kind, like my Butter Bean and Thyme dip—see photo on page 168—are excellent too): they are layered, they are often baked like my Artichoke and Spinach Dip (see page 169), and they are all sorts of yummy.

This butternut squash purée is one of those dishes that requires so little effort on the part of the cook, yet looks wonderful—perfect as a dip before supper starts. It would also be a great addition to a mezze.

I've discovered that it is also a crafty way to serve squash to the naysayers: there's something about the addition of the creamy cheese and the seeds that makes it look a whole lot more appealing than your average bowl of orange mush.

It has just three processes, the steaming of the squash, its puréeing, and the whipping of the cheese. What could be easier? (You do need a food processor for this dish.)

The purée is delicious served either hot or cold.

SECRET
Pumpkin oil is perfect for the garnish, but it's not always easy—or cheap—to find, so you can replace it with any oil with a distinct flavor. I like walnut or hazelnut, but a lovely, grassy Greek olive oil would be delicious here, too.

MAKES 1 LARGE BOWL

1 butternut squash
Olive oil
Salt and freshly ground black
  pepper
½ cup [125 g] ricotta cheese
1 Tbsp pumpkin seeds and
  pumpkin oil (or other oil with
  distinct flavor), to garnish

METHOD

Roughly chop the squash into small chunks, removing the seeds, and steam over a pan of boiling water for approximately 20 minutes.

When soft, scoop the flesh away from the skin into a food processor bowl, and pulse with a drizzle of olive oil and a pinch of salt, until a purée forms.

Put the ricotta into a bowl, and add a pinch of salt and a grind of black pepper. Whip together briefly with a fork.

To serve, spoon the purée into a flattish bowl, and carefully spoon the cheese into the middle, flattening it with the back of the spoon. Sprinkle over the seeds, and drizzle over some oil.

THE HOLIDAY SEASON PARTY

Whether your idea of a holiday season party is hosting three hundred of your closest friends in a ballroom, or having ten friends over for mulled wine and a kitchen supper, there are some tricks to make the whole shebang simpler.

Send out the invitations well in advance. That way, if people get a better offer, hopefully they will honor your request—even if they come to you first and move on. I like "Paperless Post" online, which allows you to send reminders and track RSVPs.

Don't overthink the decor: there is always the temptation to go all out at Christmas, and while I am a fan of the over-the-top event, I say save it for the rest of the year. Christmas decorations are wonderful, so I like to stay traditional, but you can always play with the color scheme if you really must be different. How about a pink tree this year?

People always eat and drink everything in sight at a holiday party. (I think they are preparing for the boredom of January by building up fat stocks.) So, if you have limited supplies, or a limited time frame, come up with a plan for politely getting people to move on to the next party, without making them feel like they are being booted out. (Turning the music down is always a good start.)

Speaking of music, a good playlist is vital. In the fluster of getting everything else organized, I always forget it. Make the music a priority—and if you don't have time, flatter a friend into doing it. Something along the lines of, "You have such amazing taste in music! Do you think ... etc, etc?"

Don't forget to tell the neighbors if your party is at home. Ideally, invite them, too, and ply them with drinks, so they can't complain if it gets a bit noisy later.

Most importantly of all, remember that the secret to hosting a good party is to enjoy yourself.

Chickpeas and flat-leaf parsley (try adding 1 Tbsp tahini and thin with warm water, to make hummus)

Chickpea, lemon, black olive, 5 Tbsp olive oil, 1 cup [100... ...emon, and flat-leaf parsley

Butter bean and thyme

BEAN PUREES

Anyone can whizz up a purée of beans or vegetables with olive oil, garlic, and herbs. It's a useful trick to know for parties: the purées can be made in advance, covered in plastic wrap, refrigerated, and then perked up with a slosh of olive oil and a scattering of herbs. Take out of the fridge an hour or so before you intend to eat.

The technique is easy: drain a can of legumes and dump into a food processor, along with a fat clove of garlic, a good pinch of salt, and some black pepper. Add a tablespoon of olive oil and whizz together until combined. Add some soft herbs for green flecks; or chili flakes for heat. Experiment with amounts of oil: a tablespoon will give you a very rough texture; 4 to 6 tablespoons poured through the lid funnel as you whizz will give you a very smooth, almost silky texture. Equally, use some of the liquid that the beans were canned in instead of extra oil.

My favorite combinations are in the photo opposite. Others you can try are cannellini bean with a little Sriracha chili sauce; roasted carrots puréed with cumin; roasted white onions puréed with ground coriander and cilantro leaves.

SUPERBOWL AVOCADO AND BEAN DIP

I cannot pretend to understand American Football, but when the annual Superbowl comes around, I see it largely as an excuse to eat vast quantities of dips and chips. So, in honor of the Superbowl and my dear friend in Chicago, the wonderful Jill, who knows as much about football as I do about fashion, here is my Superbowl Dip. It's based on nachos, but designed for easier scooping.

SERVES 6 TO 8
Refried beans
Grated cheese (Monterey Jack or cheddar)
Chopped olives
Tomato salsa

Dash of hot sauce (such as Tabasco)
Sour cream
Four-Minute Guacamole, to serve (see page 170)

METHOD
Preheat the oven to 350°F [180°C]. In a large ovenproof dish, spoon the beans, cover with grated cheese, then olives, salsa, hot sauce, and sour cream. Cover the whole lot with grated cheese. Put in the oven for 10 to 15 minutes until it is warmed through, and the cheese has melted. Spread more sour cream over the top, then smooth a layer of guacamole over it with the back of a spoon. Use salted tortilla chips for dipping. (Try not to spill down your front.)

ARTICHOKE AND SPINACH DIP

One of my favorite dips is the American classic, artichoke and spinach, a dip that I have never seen over on the English side of the Atlantic. I first had it in an East Village bar in New York, and was speechless at its addictiveness. It's a baked dip, so served hot, and is rich with tangy artichokes, cheese, cream, and spinach.

SERVES 6 TO 8
Scant 1 cup [200 g] cream cheese
⅔ cup [50 g] finely grated Parmesan cheese
⅔ cup [150 g] sour cream
2 Tbsp mayonnaise (this is optional, but do not use a reduced-fat version, as it may split)
¾ cup [200 g] frozen chopped spinach, thawed
14-oz [400-g] jar artichoke hearts, drained and finely chopped
Salt and freshly ground black pepper

METHOD
Preheat the oven to 350°F [180°C]. Put the cream cheese, Parmesan, sour cream, and mayo into a big bowl and stir until thoroughly mixed. Mix in the spinach and artichokes. Grind over lots of black pepper and add salt to taste. Transfer to an ovenproof bowl and bake for 20 minutes. Excellent with tortilla chips, pita bread, or carrot sticks.

FOUR-MINUTE GUACAMOLE

There are as many ways to make guacamole as there are varieties of avocado in Mexico. I'm not pretending that this is an authentic version, but it's still delicious. And, best of all, it takes maybe four minutes. Sold? I knew you would be.

Ideally, this is pounded with a pestle in a large mortar—or the *molcajete* in which guacamole is traditionally made. Otherwise, a bowl and the back of a fork will suffice.

SERVES 6
2 large avocados (or 4 of those baby ones)
Dash of hot sauce (Tabasco is good)
½ red onion, finely chopped
1 Tbsp lime juice (or lemon)
Good pinch of salt
1 small tomato, very finely chopped
1 leafy cilantro sprig, finely chopped,
  with stalk included

METHOD
Halve the avocados and scoop out the flesh into a mortar (or a bowl).

Add the dash of hot sauce, red onion, lime juice, salt, tomato, and cilantro.

Pound it all together with a pestle or fork. Guacamole is supposed to be chunky, so don't reduce it to pulp.

Eat with chips, or crudités, if you are inclined towards healthy eating.

Do not make in advance: guacamole is all about the fresh flavors, and it will go brown.

PIMIENTOS DE PADRÓN FRITOS

Oh, I have much love for *pimientos de Padrón fritos*. Originating from Padrón in Galicia, in the northwest corner of Spain, the dish is a trinity of little green peppers, olive oil, and kosher salt. It takes a matter of minutes to get from a rinse under the faucet to being showered with kosher salt on the plate, via a frying pan of hot oil. The perfect TV snack: no carbs, but ever so addictive and good.

However, although they do appear to be the simplest possible snack, they come with a built-in surprise. These deceptive little peppers are the Russian roulette of vegetables: for every five or so you pop in your mouth, one will be super hot. I am taking this on trust, though, because, for all the plates of pimientos de Padrón I have eaten over the years, I have not yet had a hot one.

ALLOW 3 TO 4 PEPPERS PER PERSON
1 Tbsp olive oil
Handful Padrón peppers
Coarse salt

METHOD
Heat up some standard olive oil in a frying pan, add your peppers, and cook over high heat until they begin to blister and blacken.

When you pour them out onto some paper towels, they will immediately deflate.

Sprinkle them with kosher salt and eat with your fingers (don't eat the stalks).

Eat, as I did in Jerez recently, accompanied by a lovely, chilled glass of Fino sherry.

SUPER-LONG CHEESE STRAWS

A cheese straw is a pleasing thing. Although possibly best eaten at parties over wooden floors, rather than carpets, as they do tend to shower flakes of pastry everywhere.

While it is more normal to make them quite short, for parties I like to make them about a foot long and place them in (well-scrubbed) glass vases. There's a practical reason for this: vases don't just look good, they are weighted at the base, so they don't topple over when flowers are placed in them. Because these straws are so long, you don't want the delicate pastry crashing to the floor.

MAKES APPROX. 10

1⅓ cups [100 g] grated Parmesan cheese
⅓ cup [25 g] English mustard powder
Flour, for dusting
1 lb [500 g] ready-made all-butter
  puff pastry sheets
1 egg, lightly beaten
3 baking sheets, greased

METHOD
Preheat the oven to 350°F [180°C].

Mix the Parmesan with the mustard powder.

Sprinkle flour over the work surface and lay out the pastry sheets. Roll out with a rolling pin, if necessary, to get it about ⅛ in [0.25 cm] thick. Scatter half the Parmesan mixture over half the pastry and fold over. Roll out once more with the rolling pin. Cut the pastry into long strips about ¾ in [2 cm] wide.

Brush each strip with the beaten egg, then sprinkle the rest of the Parmesan mixture over each one.

Transfer each strip to the baking sheets, twisting it twice as you lay it down. Bake for approximately 15 minutes until puffed up and golden. Remove to a wire rack to cool.

DELICIOUS LITTLE THINGS ON TOAST

JAMON, MOZZARELLA, AND BASIL ON WALNUT BREAD
Brush slices of walnut bread with olive oil and toast under the broiler on each side for a few minutes. Cut the toasted bread into fingers, place a basil leaf on each one, then a strip of jamón, followed by a small piece of mozzarella.

FIGS AND PROSCIUTTO ON SOURDOUGH
Oil and toast bread as above, lay on the prosciutto, then top with fig quarters.

MUSHROOM, CHIVE, AND CREAM CHEESE ON GRANARY
Blitz 18 oz [500 g] mushrooms in a food processor, then fry in 1 Tbsp butter until soft and the juices have evaporated. Pour into a bowl and mix with $^2/_3$ cup [150 g] cream cheese and some finely snipped chives. Pile onto toasted granary. Grind over black pepper.

ARTICHOKE PASTE ON SOURDOUGH
Whizz a jar of artichokes with their oil in a food processor, check seasoning, and spread on oiled and toasted sourdough.

SECRET
My mother always used to serve what seemed like hundreds of the goat cheese toasts at drinks parties; one of her tricks was to slice and toast the bread rounds in advance, put them in the freezer until needed, then pop them under the broiler still frozen.

GOAT CHEESE WITH PX ON TOAST

PX is short for Pedro Ximénez, one of the richest, most delicious sherries, and the raisin-y sweetness is fantastic against the sharp, creamy tang of goat cheese. Serve these as party snacks, or three at a time with some salad for a starter or light lunch. Ideally, you need to use a *bûche de chèvre*, the narrow logs of goat cheese with a rind, which come wrapped in plastic-covered paper. You could use a spreadable goat cheese, but you won't get the lovely, melted gooeyness that comes from a cheese with a rind.

They are best made using a *ficelle* (the slightly slimmer form of baguette), so you get a good ratio of cheese to bread.

SERVES 8 TO 12 AS PARTY SNACKS
2 bûches de chèvre
2 ficelles or 1 French baguette
3 generous Tbsp [50 ml] Pedro Ximénez sherry

METHOD
Unwrap the cheese and slice into ½-in [1-cm] rounds. It's easiest to use a serrated or bread knife, to prevent the cheese sticking.

Turn on the broiler to high. Slice the bread into ½-in [1-cm] thick rounds and broil on one side until golden. Flip over the rounds, place a piece of cheese on each one, and return to the broiler.

When the cheese is bubbling, remove from the broiler and brush sherry over each round.

Either slide onto boards, or serve on plates with watercress and lettuce.

THE COCKTAILS
AND PIE PARTY

My birthday falls at the beginning of December. For someone who loves to throw a party, this is not exactly ideal, given that it's party month. Even if people aren't flitting from event to event, they are likely to be wound up with the excitement and stress of preparing for the Christmas season.

On the other hand, my birthday is early enough to kick off the holiday season. After a few parties that I have filed under "trial and error," I have finally got my perfect holiday party recipe down pat.

The most important thing is to make sure that you don't leave yourself with too much to do during the party itself: the key to a good time is preparation, preparation, preparation.

The first thing I learned was, no fiddly canapés. For my thirtieth I had planned a menu of trays of simple little things to eat, but hadn't given much thought to how they were going to be assembled during the actual party. I didn't have any help in the kitchen, bar my roommate, and it was all a little bit disastrous. I had also planned that my boyfriend and I would serve all the drinks. No, that didn't really work either. Because someone needs to answer the door, take coats, and welcome guests.

I learned my lesson from that event: henceforth I would always have somebody to help me with, well, everything. If you are partner-free, then two people. So the most important thing is to secure your help well in advance. I recommend asking at your local bar for recommendations.

Drinks-wise, it's best to keep it simple. No one really likes punch after university (and did we even like it then?), and unless you are standing outside to watch fireworks or sing carols, resist the temptation to serve mulled wine.

I usually serve cocktails and Champagne or prosecco only, having searched around online for the best deal, and then having the retailer deliver it to me, to save me hefting it into the house. I ban red wine: there's always a spillage disaster however hard you try to contain it.

While I love the idea of having somebody doing a Tom Cruise and shaking individually made cocktails over their shoulder, in reality it is not very practical if you've only got one bar person and fifty people desperate for a drink. So what we do is stick to one spirit, usually vodka (because most people drink it), and make up several pitchers of cocktails in advance. (A pre-party cocktail-tasting supper, a week or so before, is clearly vital.)

Ice in large quantity is essential—keep it in the bath if necessary. Serve the pre-mixed cocktails over ice in a highball, or shake them up with ice on demand. Place buckets filled with ice and water under the bar table for the Champagne or prosecco.

Don't forget that you'll need plenty of soft drinks: my favorite is huge pitchers of elderflower syrup with lots of mint and ice to make them look pretty.

After my canapé disaster, I decided to stop serving fiddly food that gets ground into carpets, and to make pies. Yes, pies. For about a hundred people, I make five giant chicken-and-vegetable pies (see page 175) and one Quorn-and-mushroom one, in roasting pans, the day before.

This is my idea of perfect party food: the already-made pies go in the oven around 7:30 P.M. to warm through. Everybody arrives at about 8 P.M. after work because they took too long getting ready, or because they are waiting for a babysitter. At 9 P.M. when everyone has had plenty of cocktails and is feeling pretty hungry, we dish up the pies onto paper plates. Everybody dives in: honestly, they couldn't be happier (who doesn't like pie?) and the best bit is that all the paper plates and plastic forks go straight into the trash, and there is no washing up.

Then, a while later, I hand around great piles of brownies (see page 150), which I have cut up in advance and plastic-wrapped.

Result: very happy guests and (almost) stress-free host.

GIANT CHICKEN PIE

Making a large pie can seem daunting, but wonderfully, it's actually rather simple, requiring nothing more complicated than a standard roasting pan. I chose the pan, as opposed to a traditional china dish, for two reasons: when I first threw a party for 100 people and wanted to feed everyone pie, I needed five or six identical dishes, and that presented two problems: cost, and storage afterwards. Then I hit on the idea of using metal roasting pans because they can be picked up for a few dollars each and they stack together. They also conduct heat beautifully, so your pie hots up rapidly.

Using a roasting pan does mean the pie isn't particularly deep, but when you are catering for the masses, you want more acreage than depth, more pastry than filling, otherwise portion control can be tricky. (Those lovely blackbird pie funnels, traditionally used in deep pies to let the steam out and stop the lid sinking, are more for decoration here than utility.)

SERVES 12 TO 15

For the poached chicken

1 organic, free-range
   chicken (around 2¾ to 3¼ lb
   [1.2 to 1.5 kg])
1 carrot
1 onion
1 leek

For the pie

4 cups [500 g] white
   mushrooms, quartered
4 leeks, thickly sliced
2 Tbsp olive oil
4 carrots, cut into chunks
¾ cup [100 g] all-purpose flour,
   plus extra for dusting
1½ lb [750 g] ready-made puff
   pastry sheets
7 Tbsp [100 g] butter
1 Tbsp Dijon mustard
4½ cups [1 L] hot liquid
   (preferably 2 cups [500 ml]
   chicken stock and 2 cups
   [500 ml] milk)
2½ cups [250 g] grated cheese
   (preferably Monterey Jack or
   cheddar)
1 egg, lightly beaten
large roasting pan

METHOD

Follow the instructions for poaching the chicken on page 73, straining and reserving the cooking liquid. Remove the meat from the bones (discarding the bones) and cut into bite-size pieces.

For the pie, fry the mushrooms and the leeks separately in 1 Tbsp olive oil each, and steam or boil the carrots until al dente. Set aside.

Sprinkle flour over the work surface and lay out the puff pastry sheets. Using the top of the roasting pan as a template, roll out the pastry further with a rolling pin (being careful not to roll it too thin) until it's big enough to fit over the pan. Using the remaining pastry, cut long strips the width and length of the lip of the roasting pan sides, to cover each side. Cover with a dish towel.

Using the butter, ¾ cup [100 g] flour, the mustard, and hot liquid, make the white sauce according to the instructions on page 73, adding in the grated cheese at the end, and stirring until melted.

Put the mushrooms, leeks, and carrots in the roasting pan, being careful not to add the cooking liquid, as this will make the sauce too runny and cause it to separate. Add the chicken and distribute evenly. Pour the white sauce over the chicken and vegetables, making sure it is mixed in. If you are using blackbird pie funnels, place these now. Let cool slightly. Preheat the oven to 350°F [180°C].

Flip the large piece of pastry over the roasting pan, using a small sharp knife to make a cross where each blackbird will poke through. Do not worry if the pastry doesn't quite stretch over the lip of the pan. Brush the beaten egg over the edges and place the pastry strips, cut earlier, over the lip of the pan to secure the pastry sheet on all sides. Brush the entire top of the pie with beaten egg.

Bake for about 25 minutes, or until the pastry is risen and golden.

BOARDS OF GOOD THINGS

I like to finish off a meal by plonking a wooden board in the middle of the table. On it will be something delicious to pick at while the conversation flows. Perhaps cheese and good bread, or maybe a selection of sweet things I have picked up on my travels. Boards of good things are great for parties, too: easy to hand around, unbreakable, and aesthetically pleasing.

There's a common fallacy that says serving up things you haven't made yourself is cheating somehow. I say pah! to that: while I would never give a TV dinner to anyone except myself (yes, sometimes the microwave is my friend), there's nothing wrong in saving yourself stress by not making everything, or skipping a course.

The most obvious thing that looks wonderful on a large board is a gorgeous, large piece of cheese. Unless you are catering for fifteen-plus people, I think it's a bit of a waste to serve up more than two types as, invariably, you will be left with plastic-wrapped pieces which lurk in the back of the fridge. Instead, invest in a showstopper piece of runny cheese such as Brie or Epoisses; or a huge hunk of hard cheese such as a farmhouse cheddar. Add grapes, dried apricots, chutney, or membrillo.

When I am abroad, I always try to find a local store to pick up local, sweet specialties for my pantry. I also do a supermarket sweep around duty-free stores when I haven't had time to go anywhere beyond hotel and meetings: even the Eurostar terminal at Gare du Nord has turned up trumps before, and it's handy having a stockpile for emergency entertaining.

These sweet things might include several types of turrón; pretty, pastel-colored Turkish delight; amaretti cookies in delicate tissue wrappers; sticky Medjool dates; broken-off pieces of panforte di Siena; biscotti; marrons glacés, and macaroons.

Delicious Things
to Buy in Spain

Spain's markets are packed full of ingredients that any greedy cook will long to buy. Fortunately, you can bring any fruit, vegetables, meat, dairy, or other animal products (such as fish, eggs, and honey) into the UK if you're traveling from a country within the EU, so if you have room in your luggage, the only issue will be the size of your purse—and your wallet.

If I have room in my hand luggage, I buy tomatoes—Spanish ones are the best in the world—and in the fall I look for interesting mushrooms.

My favorite Spanish market is the nineteenth-century Mercat de Sant Josep de la Boqueria on Barcelona's Ramblas (see right).

Even if I only have a few spare minutes in the city, I always try to buy a selection of technicolored glacé fruits from one of the many specialists in the Boqueria. They are wonderful as an after-dinner treat, used in Christmas cake, or chopped into ice cream to make scrumptious tutti frutti.

Unfortunately, Americans will have to curtail purchases of fresh fruit and veg and other produce.

I always try to go home with some of the following:

- Pimientos de Padrón
- Dried chilies
- Chorizo sausages
- Jamón serrano
- Salted Marcona almonds
- Turrón—the chewy Spanish nougat, which is especially good covered in chocolate
- Polvorones—crumbly almond cookies
- Glacé fruits

Spanish Markets to Look out for

Mercat de Sant Josep de la Boqueria (also known as La Boqueria) on Barcelona's Ramblas; open Monday to Saturday 8 A.M. to 8:30 PM; www.boqueria.info

Mercado Central de Abastos, Plaza de Abastos, Jerez de la Frontera; www.jerez.es

Mercado de San Miguel, Plaza de San Miguel, Madrid; open Monday to Wednesday and Sunday, 10 A.M. to midnight; Thursday to Saturday, 10 A.M. to 2 P.M.; www.mercadodesanmiguel.es

BANG BANG CHICKEN

I don't just love this dish because of its name (which is irresistibly good and comes from the noise made when cooks would tenderize the chicken by banging it with a mallet) but because it is as finger-lickin' good as it is easy. It's so simple that it would be a great recipe to make with children, although there is nothing childish about it. It originates from Sichuan, where the inclusion of Sichuan peppercorns makes it a much fierier dish than we eat in the West. (Feel free to add 1 or 2 tsp if you crave the burn.)

Bang bang chicken is usually served with its sauce over noodles—either rice or mung bean—but I like to serve mine as a DIY version with all the ingredients separated, so the eaters can choose their favorite combination to roll up in a pancake.

I first made this for a Shrove Tuesday (Mardi Gras) supper party, which I didn't want to feel like a one-note meal, so I used a different kind of pancake for each course. The ones I use to wrap the chicken in are the thin, rice versions that you can find in any Asian supermarket, often in the freezer section. They are inexpensive and are packaged so that you can just remove what you need, and put the others back in the freezer. (I find them very useful for last-minute suppers.)

SERVES 6

6 chicken breasts (on the bone)
7 oz [200 g] rice noodles
Sesame oil

For the sauce
½ cup [8 Tbsp] peanut butter
  (either smooth or crunchy)
Generous ⅓ cup [6 Tbsp] sweet
  chili sauce
2 tsp lime juice
2 Tbsp soy sauce
2 Tbsp rice vinegar
2 Tbsp sesame oil

For the table
4 rice pancakes per head, plus
  a few extra (about 30)
3 Tbsp sesame seeds
2 cups [200 g] bean sprouts
2 carrots (optional)
2 baby Gem or romaine lettuces
Bunch scallions
1 to 2 cucumbers
½ bunch cilantro

METHOD

Rinse the chicken breasts under a running faucet. Put them in a saucepan, cover with cold water, and place over medium heat. Bring to a simmer and poach gently for 15 minutes. Check the inside of a breast, and if there is any hint of pinkness, simmer for another 5 minutes, or until cooked through.

When the chicken is cooked, remove from the water, take off the skin, and discard. Reserve the poaching liquid. Pull the meat from the bone and shred neatly—you can use a fork or your fingers.

Dump the sauce ingredients in another pan with 1 cup [240 ml] of the reserved poaching liquid. Mix thoroughly and heat over gentle heat to warm through. (Do not to let it burn—burnt peanuts smell revolting.)

Plunge the rice noodles into a pan of boiling water. They should cook almost immediately, but do check package instructions. Drain, then add a drop of sesame oil to stop them sticking together.

If you have a steamer, place it over a pan of simmering water, and add the pancakes to the basket to warm through. Otherwise, they can be wrapped in foil and warmed in the oven.

Heat a frying pan and pour in the sesame seeds to toast for 30 seconds. (This is optional, but they taste better toasted.)

For the table, rinse the bean sprouts, grate the carrots, if using, separate the lettuce leaves, shred the onions, and cut the cucumber into matchsticks.

Arrange the chicken, noodles, pancakes, vegetables, and cilantro on a series of plates. Pour the sauce into 2 bowls. Put the sesame seeds in a little bowl. Let everyone assemble their own pancakes at the table. Don't forget lots of napkins, as the sauce drips down chins and fingers.

(If you are making this on a hot summer day, don't heat the sauce and allow the chicken and the noodles to cool to room temperature.)

DIY SALMON AND VEGETABLE PARCELS
WITH LEMON AND CREAM SAUCE

There is something very beguiling about brown paper parcels tied up with string—as we all know from the song. And, while I'm always happy to find a present inside, a delicious meal is equally welcome.

I first came across this way of serving food *en papillote* at a very smart lunch in a marquee. Running down the center of the table were pots of soft green herbs, and each place setting had a little pitcher of creamy sauce and a pair of scissors. The idea was that we would open up our parcels, pour over the sauce and snip the herbs of our choice over the top. It's a lovely idea, and easily replicated at home with little fuss. I cook both salmon and vegetables this way, and even if there are no vegetarians around, cook several green parcels as well, to accompany the fish.

METHOD
Preheat the oven to 350°F [180°C].

For the lemon and cream sauce, cook the shallot, lemon juice, and wine together at a gentle simmer for 10 to 15 minutes until it has reduced by half. Add the cream and cook for another 5 minutes. Add the butter cubes to the sauce, piece by piece, vigorously whisking each time until all the butter is combined. Do be careful it doesn't burn.

Place the salmon fillet or the vegetables in the middle of a square of parchment paper, and add a bit of butter and a splash of white wine. Wrap up the parchment to form a parcel. Secure with twine, repeat with the remaining salmon and vegetables, and place on a large baking sheet in the oven. Cook for about 10 minutes. Use a spatula to remove the parcels from the baking sheet, as the liquid inside will make the parcels floppy.

Serve the parcels on a large platter in the middle of the table for everyone to help themselves. Then they can snip their own herbs, squeeze over a lemon wedge, and pour over the lemon and cream sauce.

SERVES 4

For the lemon and cream sauce
1 shallot, very finely chopped
Juice of 2 lemons
2 Tbsp white wine
1 cup [250 ml] light cream
1 cup + 2 Tbsp [250 g] butter, cubed

For the fish parcels
1 salmon fillet per person
1 Tbsp butter
2 Tbsp white wine
Parchment paper
Kitchen twine

For the vegetable parcels
Petite sweet peas, snow peas, sugar snap peas, green beans, trimmed asparagus, julienned carrots, zucchini, and fennel
1 Tbsp butter
2 Tbsp white wine
Parchment paper
Kitchen twine

For the table
Fresh chervil, chives, tarragon, flat-leaf parsley, thyme, oregano, dill
Lemon wedges

BAKED CAMEMBERT
WITH HERBS AND ROASTED SCALLIONS

Is this a recipe? I think that's probably pushing it. What it is, is a brilliant way of turning unripe Camembert—the type that seems to have a Styrofoam middle—into a meltingly unctuous dish that far transcends its rather dull origins.

A couple of these are perfect to plonk on the table pre-supper, when guests arrive ravenous, but food isn't quite ready. Or else, you can serve one each as an entrée alongside some good bread, or a bowl of boiled potatoes. Cornichons (gherkins) are a perfect accompaniment.

Any sprigs of herbs will do: rosemary or thyme are lovely; equally, marjoram and oregano work well. You could also try trickling over some honey, as its sweetness contrasts beautifully with the salty, creamy cheese.

I like to accompany the cheese with bunches of scallions, roasted in the oven at the same time. Do make sure you buy the Camemberts in wooden boxes, not cardboard ones, as the latter will leak molten goop.

SERVES 2 TO 6, DEPENDING ON HUNGER LEVELS
1 bunch scallions
1 Tbsp olive oil, plus more
  for drizzling
1 Camembert in a wooden box
Few sprigs of herbs

METHOD
Preheat the oven to 350°F [180°C].

Snip off each end of the scallions and place in an ovenproof dish with the oil and toss together.

Unwrap the Camembert and discard the lid of the box. Make 3 slits in the cheese, poke in sprigs of herbs, and drizzle over some olive oil to keep the crust supple during the cooking.

Whack the boxed cheese in the oven, alongside the scallions, in a big dish for about 15 minutes. (Do not ever bake just in their boxes. You are risking a big molten-cheese mess on the floor of your oven.)

The scallions will need about 20 minutes altogether, or until soft with crispy—even blackened—ends.

QUESO FUNDIDO

I always love the idea of sitting around a big steaming dish of food, into which we can all dive, elbows out and forks in—and if it involves melted cheese, then so much the better.

Queso fundido (meaning "melted cheese") is the Mexican cousin of Swiss fondue. Although you don't dip anything in the cheese, it does make sense to keep it warming over a lamp or tea light, as you would a fondue, so that the cheese doesn't seize and separate.

It's worth trying to track down some of the traditional cheeses that are used to make this dish, including Oaxaca and Chihuahua. However, the rest of us can get by just fine using a mixture of mozzarella and a hard, tasty cheese.

SECRET

For a vegetarian variation, omit the chorizo, heat 1 Tbsp butter, and add a crushed garlic clove and 10 oz [300 g] sliced mushrooms. Cook until soft and pour over the bubbling cheese.

SERVES 4 TO 6

1 cup [200 g] finely chopped chorizo

4 tomatoes

1 medium onion, chopped

1 large garlic clove, finely chopped

5 cups [500 g] grated cheese (my basic mix is 2½ cups [250 g] grated mozzarella plus 2½ cups [250 g] grated Monterey Jack. If I have some Manchego left over from a party, then I sub that in, too. Mmm.)

Handful cilantro leaves

Corn tortilla chips or large tortillas, to serve

Large ovenproof frying pan, preferably cast iron

METHOD

Place a frying pan over medium-high heat. Add the chorizo. (Do not add any extra oil: it gives off plenty.) Cook for about 5 minutes, until it starts to give off its characteristic red oil. Then remove the chorizo with a slotted spoon to a plate, leaving the oil in the pan.

While the chorizo is cooking, chop the tomatoes into small pieces.

Keep the pan over the heat, but turn it down to medium. Add the chopped onion, and cook until translucent. This will take at least 15 minutes. When the onion is done, add the garlic and cook for a few minutes. Then put the chorizo back in the pan, make sure everything is mixed together, and keep warm over very low heat.

Meanwhile, preheat the oven to 350°F [180°C]. Mix the cheeses together and add to the cast iron frying pan. Stick in the oven for 5 to 10 minutes, but keep a beady eye on the cheese: you don't want it starting to separate. (The aim is a pan of molten deliciousness.) Remove the pan from the oven and spoon the warm chorizo-onion mixture in the middle.

Heap over the chopped tomatoes and scatter lots of cilantro over everything. Either dip tortilla chips into the melted cheese, or spoon the cheese onto large corn or wheat tortillas.

Favorite Florists

I love sending people flowers, and I love receiving them too, so I've always figured if sending them gives even half the joy I get from an unsolicited bunch of flowers, then it's money well spent.

These are the people from whom I order flowers around the world.

Paris: L'Artisan Fleuriste

Their beautiful, color coordinated shop in the Marais is wonderful to visit, but their insistence on seasonal, and usually French flowers makes for glorious bouquets too.

95 Rue Vieille du Temple, 75003 Paris

Sydney: Mr Cook

Order a massed bunch of just one bloom from Sean Cook for maximum impact.

318 New South Head Rd, Double Bay, Sydney, NSW 2028 www.mrcook.com.au

New York: Opalia Flowers

Beautiful Opalia in Boerum Hill, Brooklyn designs the most ravishing vases—in season ask for their blowsy peonies—and delivers all over the five boroughs.

377 Atlantic Avenue, Brooklyn, NY 11217 www.opaliaflowers.com

UK: Rebel Rebel

I use Rebel Rebel to send flowers to my friends in East London and each time they come up with something perfectly custom-made for the recipient.

5 Broadway Market, London E8 4PH www.rebelrebel.co.uk

UK: Miss Pickering

Whether she uses herbs or flowers, Miss Pickering's scented arrangements are always a joy to behold. She also has a wonderful whippet guarding her shop.

7 St Paul's Street, Stamford PE9 2BE www.misspickering.com

ICE CREAM SUNDAES

Why should ice cream sundaes be just for children? There's a voluptuous pleasure in a loaded spoonful of ice cream, covered in a scrumptious sauce, and loaded with nuts, topped with, maybe, a flump of whipped cream. Just make sure you forget storebought, luminous syrups; use proper chocolate in your sauce; fresh fruit, not canned; and avoid squirty cream, which always disappointingly melts to a watery nothingness.

BANANA SPLIT
This is sundae simplicity at its best: take one banana, peel it, halve it lengthwise, spoon vanilla ice cream down the middle, drizzle over hot chocolate sauce, cover in whipped cream and toasted almonds.

HOT FUDGE SUNDAE
Two scoops of vanilla ice cream, topped with hot fudge sauce, whipped cream, toasted almonds, and a cherry on top.

HOT BROWNIE SUNDAE
A warm brownie (preferably straight from the oven—see page 150), on which are balanced two scoops of either vanilla or chocolate ice cream, butterscotch sauce, whipped cream, and maple walnuts.

KNICKERBOCKER GLORY
Experts believe that a classic Knickerbocker is served in a tall glass, filled with layers of three scoops of different colors (traditionally strawberry, chocolate, and vanilla), jelly, chopped fruit and nuts, chocolate sauce, strawberry sauce, and toasted almonds. A cherry on the top, preferably one from a jar, is obligatory.

BROWN DERBY
A sugared ring donut, topped with a swirl of ice cream, chocolate sauce, and chopped nuts appeared on Wimpy (a UK burger chain) menus throughout my childhood. I was never allowed to order one, but I made up for the deprivation by constructing one recently. It was epic.

UNBEATABLE ACCOMPANIMENTS FOR VANILLA ICE CREAM
Blueberries and lemon curd

Strawberry purée, crushed meringue, slivered almonds

Hazelnut chocolate spread, chopped nuts, hot chocolate sauce

Mango purée, sliced peaches, and whipped cream

GREAT SUNDAE TOPPINGS

Chocolate sauce

Butterscotch sauce

Marshmallow creme

Teeny, tiny marshmallows

Sprinkles

Nonpareils

Chocolate chips

Honey

Maple syrup

Bananas

Whipped cream

Strawberry purée

Mango purée

Raspberry coulis

Sliced peaches

Chantilly cream

Chopped nuts

Slivered almonds

Candied walnuts

Berries (blueberries, chopped strawberries, raspberries, blackberries, black currants)

Rose syrup

Hazelnut chocolate spread

Lemon curd

TOP PLACES TO INDULGE IN

Ice Cream
AND *Sundaes*
AROUND THE WORLD

UK

The Parlour Restaurant at Fortnum & Mason, 181 Piccadilly, London W1A 1ER

Gelupo, 7 Archer Street, London W1D 7AU

Chin Chin Laboratorists, 49–50 Camden Lock Place, London NW1 8AF

Marine Ices, 8 Haverstock Hill, London NW3 2BL

Ice Cream Parlour at Harrods, 2nd floor, Harrods, 87–135 Brompton Road, London SW1X 7XL

Roskilly Ice Cream, Tregellast Barton Farm, St Keverne, Helston, Cornwall TR12 6NX

Morelli's, 14 Victoria Parade, Broadstairs, Kent CT10 1QS

Nardini's Esplanade Café, 2 Greenock Rd, Largs, North Ayrshire KA30 8NF

USA

Serendipity 3, 225 East 60th Street, New York, NY 10022

Ici Ice Cream, 2948 College Avenue, Berkeley, CA 94705

The Ice Cream Bar, 815 Cole Street, Cole Valley, San Francisco, CA 94117

FRANCE

Berthillon, 31 rue Saint Louis en l'Île, 75004 Paris

SINGAPORE

Azabu Sabo, Food Court @ Takashimaya Department Store, 391 Orchard Road, Singapore 238873

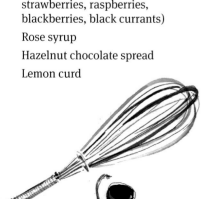

INDEX

ACKNOWLEDGMENTS

My list of people to thank was so long that it was in danger of forming a chapter in itself. Since I started LibertyLondonGirl in 2006, I have been astonished by both the kindness of friends and the support of strangers, not least from within the blogging community.

I'd like to thank my readers, without whom this book would not have been possible. It was their thousands of Tweets, comments, and emails asking when I was publishing a cookbook that spurred me on to finishing the recipe book I had first started writing in 2001.

There has always been food on the blog, but it wasn't until 2009 when two men and two Basset Hounds from Colts Neck, New Jersey swooped into Manhattan in their SUV and kidnapped me for the summer (which turned into fall) that I really started to focus on writing recipes on LLG. So to my darlings: Jason Grenfell-Gardner and Yoann Ricau, and Max and Finchley, thank you for the support, the kickass kitchen, and the picking up of the grocery bills.

There would have been no book at all without the extraordinary team at Quadrille. Extra special shiny thanks to Jane O'Shea, to my editor Céline Hughes, who has the patience of several saints, to Nicola Ellis, who designs like a dream, and to the wonderful Ed Griffiths who knows what's what.

Curtis Brown in London have held my hand all the way. Without my first agent and dear friend Richard Gibb, whose unwavering faith in me gave me faith in myself, and my literary agent, the ineffable Gordon Wise, who kicks me into touch with much charm, *FFF* would never have made the leap from my head to paper. Likewise my crack CB agent-ing team: Jacquie Drewe, Vanessa Fogarty, and Fran Linke, and Team LLG: Briony Whitehouse, Katie Bowkett, Katie Rose, and, most importantly, Emily Cunningham, have all helped me turn LLG into my second career.

I would like to thank Jane Bruton and Hattie Brett for helping me give up my blogging anonymity in the pages of *Grazia*, and launching me on this adventure in such inimitable style.

Jackie Dixon for making me move to New York in the first place, and for the sterling friends I made in my years in the city. Not least Rachel Carroll, Shayne Ebudo, Judy Kim, Jill Mahmarian-Fields, and Carol-Anne Turner. You guys kept my head above water mentally and physically, and I will never forget it.

My life would be a barren place without my girlfriends. In particular I want to thank the ones who have helped me get this book finished, from recipe testing to gin consumption. They are Brigitte Atkinson, Meriel Bruce, Anne Fousse, Hannah Hayes-Westall, Ayla Master, Clare Shaw, Tara Spring, and Philippa Wright.

Launching a blog, and then a business on your own, with no money or external investment at the beginning—and then keeping it going for eight years now—equals a lot of highs and lows. There have been some wonderful people who, although they may not have realized it, gave me the oompf to carry on. So thank you variously for support, advice, commissions, belief, and press coverage: Sam Baker, Navaz Batliwalla, Helen Brocklebank, Colin Byrne, Josie Carol, Hannah Clifford, and all at Wild Card PR, Suzannah Crabbe, Michael Donovan, John Franklin, Kara Goodley and her team, Saska Graville, Seth Haberman, Jane Harper, Lizzie Harper, Laurent Kretz, India Knight, Helena Lang, Lauren Laverne, Sadie Mantovani, Diana Massey, Louisa McCarthy, Jenny McLaughlin, Virginia Norris, Caroline Perham, Lucy Perceval, Lucinda Pride, Liz Roscoe, Baukjen de Swaan Arons, Matt Rudd, Beth Schepens, Amanda Selby, Lauren Sherman, Richard Storer, and Anna Vale.

And last but not least, Peter Beckett, Elizabeth Cochrane, Joanna Richmond, Russell Taylor (who first encouraged me to write a cookbook all those years ago), Chloe Beeney, Tony Borer and Barrie Dougdale, Rosalind Crossman, Rachel Eastwood, Mark Hayes-Westall, Lisa Lamb, Michele Law and Henry Knowles, Maria, Emily Moore, Sarah Miller, Emma Mosley, Rodger and Christine Newman, Rollo Ross, Laetitia Rutherford, Bumble Ward, Justine Ragany, Philip Shaw, Vicky Silverthorn, Dave Smith, Athena Skouvakis, Francesca Todd, John Waterlow, and Julian Shah-Tayler.

Thank you to Green Pan, Lavenham, Billington's, Green & Blacks, Le Creuset, Kenwood, Nespresso, and Sevket Gokce at Parkway Greens for their support during the writing of this book.